welcome

I've been on a quest to find inner peace since 2004 after I lost my girlfriend in a car accident.

I've read everything from Eastern and Western philosophies. From Thoreau, Cicero, Osho, and Plato. From Rumi, Krishnamurti, and Gandhi. From Seneca, Mother Teresa, Swami Vivekananda, and Buddha.

You may feel overwhelmed, chronically stressed, and confused. But with the right mindset and perspective, you can say goodbye to these feelings.

Join me as we navigate toward a better life with the best quotes, ideas, and insights I've gathered in the last 20 years.

Life is uphill, but it can also be peaceful.

table of contents

part 1

inner peace

What is inner peace? How can you have more of it?
Why should you work toward it?

Inner peace by being present

JUST DRINK YOUR TEA

Once there was a wise old monk named Thich Nhat Hanh, who taught the world about the art of acceptance and inner peace. In his early years, he witnessed the turmoil of war in Vietnam but remained dedicated in his belief in peace.

One day, a woman approached Thich Nhat Hanh, overwhelmed by her anger and despair over the war. She begged him for guidance on how to find peace amidst the chaos.

Thich Nhat Hanh listened quietly and then offered her a simple yet profound lesson. He handed her a cup of tea and said, "Before you drink your tea, think only of drinking your tea. Let go of your worries about the past and future. Be fully present in this moment."

The woman followed his advice, focusing solely on the warmth of the cup, the aroma of the tea, and the sensation of each sip. In that moment, she found a sense of calm she hadn't felt in years.

Neither seek nor avoid, take what comes. Swami Vivekananda

an open mind

Empty your mind, be formless, shapeless, like water. Bruce Lee

Quiet mind, easy life. Busy mind, hard life. Maxime Lagacé

Have a mind that is open to everything, and attached to nothing. Tilopa

Inner peace is when you stop rejecting your current state. Maxime Lagacé

stay free

Those who are free of resentful thoughts
surely find peace.

Buddha

be indifferent

IT'S OUTSIDE OF YOUR CONTROL

A rational person can find peace
by cultivating indifference to
things outside of their control.
Naval Ravikant

IT'S NATURAL

You'll have peace when you're ok
with not being ok. James Pierce

IT'S AN EXTERNAL EVENT

Indifference to external events.
And a commitment to justice in
your own acts. Marcus Aurelius

Learning to ignore things is one of the great paths to inner peace. Robert J. Sawyer

remain cool, calm

This is my secret. I don't mind what happens. Jiddu Krishnamurti

Inner peace is when you accept most things. Overwhelm is when you care for most things. Maxime Lagacé

Inner peace is beyond victory or defeat. Bhagavad Gita

Anyone who enjoys inner peace is no more broken by failure than he is inflated by success. Matthieu Ricard

peace from within

Each one has to find his peace from within. And peace to be real must be unaffected by outside circumstances.

Ralph Waldo Emerson

no comparison

There is "what is" only when there is no comparison at all,
and to live with what is, is to be peaceful.

Bruce Lee

stay light

Peace is when you lean into what's happening. Maxime Lagacé

It's a nice feeling to just be. Pema Chödrön

Wherever you go, there you are. Jon Kabat-Zinn

Freedom from desire leads to inner peace. Lao Tzu

key takeaways

DO'S

 Learn to discern what's important and what's not. Then focus on the former.

 Think "slow and steady". Life is smoother that way.

 Focus on things you control: how much you work, how you react, how you treat others, where you put your attention, what are your habits, etc.

DONT'S

 Don't focus on things you don't control (what people say or do, the weather, your past, etc.).

 Don't resist the moment. Accept it. Deal with it. Then move on.

 Don't get attached to outcomes. Just focus on doing your best today.

part 2

acceptance &
letting go

What does it mean to let go? What is acceptance?
Why should you practice it? Indeed, it's hard to be
peaceful if you hold on and resist the way things are.

14

Inner peace through acceptance

DON'T FIGHT FATE, ACCEPT IT

Famous composer Ludwig van Beethoven started losing his hearing in his late 20s, the unimaginable for a musician.

He thought about giving up composing entirely. But then, he thought to himself, "I will take fate by the throat."

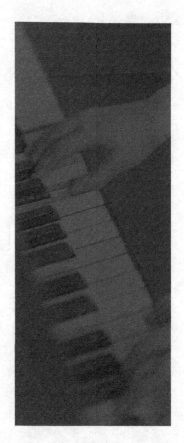

Beethoven didn't magically regain his hearing, but he accepted his reality. He found new ways to compose, using internal visualizations of the music.

This acceptance opened doors. It led to some of his most profound works, filled with a raw power and emotional depth.

Beethoven's story shows that acceptance isn't about resignation. It's about finding a way to thrive despite challenges, and sometimes, letting go of what you can't control allows you to create something truly extraordinary.

Surrender to what is. Let go of what was. Have faith in what will be.
Sonia Ricotti

no expectations

Give up your attachment to having things your way. Iyanla Vanzant

Letting go doesn't mean you give up. It means you keep going but you're indifferent to results. Maxime Lagacé

Peace begins when expectation ends. Sri Chinmoy

When you become a lover of what is, the war is over. Byron Katie

Seek not that the things
which happen should
happen as you wish; but
wish the things which
happen to be as they are,
and you will have a tranquil
flow of life. Epictetus

don't fight

HAPPINESS EXISTS
Happiness can exist only in
acceptance. George Orwell

IT'S YOUR CHOICE
Whatever the present moment
contains, accept it as if you had
chosen it. Eckhart Tolle

DON'T RESIST
When the resistance is gone, so
are the demons. Pema Chödrön

First, you accept.
Then, you become
peaceful.

acceptance vs expectations

My happiness grows in direct proportion
to my acceptance,
and in inverse proportion
to my expectations.

Michael J. Fox

how you feel is fine

Whatever state I am in, I see it as a state of
mind to be accepted as it is.

Nisargadatta Maharaj

stay serene

Whatever comes, don't push it away.
When it goes, do not grieve.

Mooji

this is reality

Let reality be reality. Let things flow naturally forward in whatever way they like. Lao Tzu

Let go of the battle. Breathe quietly and let it be. Let your body relax and your heart soften. Open to whatever you experience without fighting. Jack Kornfield

Reality hurts when you fight it. It makes you strong when you accept it. Maxime Lagacé

THINK ABOUT THAT

Celebration is my attitude, unconditional to what life brings. Osho

When we stop opposing reality, action becomes simple, fluid, kind, and fearless. Byron Katie

stillness

Real happiness only comes as a side-effect of peace. Most of it is going to come from acceptance, not from changing your external environment. Naval Ravikant

If you let go a little you will have a little peace. If you let go a lot you will have a lot of peace. Ajahn Chah

It is inner stillness that will save and transform the world. Eckhart Tolle

key takeaways

DO'S

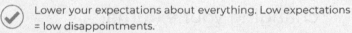 Lower your expectations about everything. Low expectations = low disappointments.

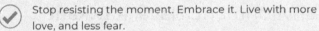 Stop resisting the moment. Embrace it. Live with more love, and less fear.

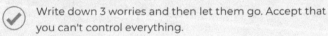 Write down 3 worries and then let them go. Accept that you can't control everything.

DONT'S

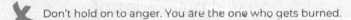 Don't hold on to anger. You are the one who gets burned.

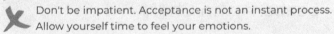 Don't be impatient. Acceptance is not an instant process. Allow yourself time to feel your emotions.

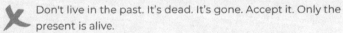 Don't live in the past. It's dead. It's gone. Accept it. Only the present is alive.

part 3

balance & harmony

Inner peace is about balance and harmony.
It's about trusting life and being fine with the
way things are. It's about moderation in your
efforts so you don't feel overwhelmed.

27

Inner peace through balance

FAST, SLOW – FLEXIBLE, SOLID

<u>Claude Monet</u> was known for his beautiful Impressionist paintings, bursting with light and color. But his early career wasn't easy. Critics slammed his work as unfinished and messy.

Discouraged, Monet retreated to the French countryside. There, he started painting outdoors, capturing the fleeting effects of sunlight on landscapes. He realized that capturing the essence of a scene, not every detail, was key.

This shift in focus brought balance to his work. He balanced capturing the beauty of the world with his own artistic vision. His paintings became more about the feeling a scene evoked, rather than a photorealistic image.

In sum, Monet's story reminds you that finding balance is an art form in itself. It's about embracing both precision and looseness, structure and flow. When you find this balance in your life, you can create something truly special, and experience a greater sense of peace and harmony.

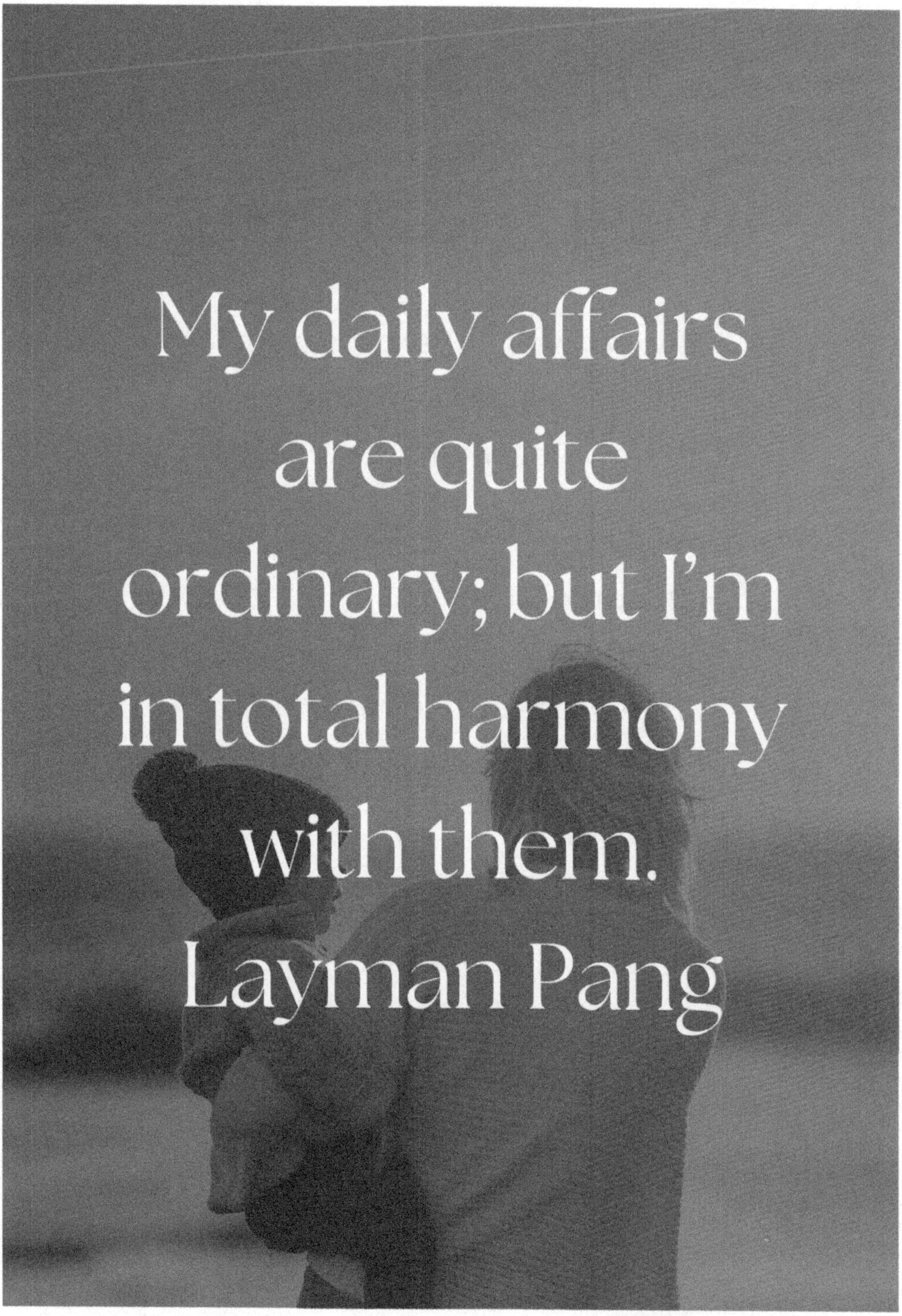

My daily affairs
are quite
ordinary; but I'm
in total harmony
with them.
Layman Pang

live in harmony

He who lives in harmony with himself lives in harmony with the universe. Marcus Aurelius

Harmony is the feeling that arises from not wanting to be somewhere else, doing something else. Raj Raghunathan

To be in harmony with the wholeness of things is not to have anxiety over imperfections. Dogen

Some of us think holding on
makes us strong
but sometimes it is letting go.
Hermann Hesse

life in balance

REST, THEN MOVE
Life is a balance between rest and movement. Osho

DO NOTHING
Sometimes it's perfectly okay, and absolutely necessary, to shut down, kick back, and do nothing. Lori Deschene

CHOOSE CAREFULLY
Life is a balance of holding on and letting go. Rumi

Retire to the center of your being, which is calmness. Paramahansa Yogananda

simplicity

The key to finding a happy balance in modern life
is simplicity.

Sogyal Rinpoche

work, love, play

Work, love and play are the great
balance wheels of man's being.

Orison Swett Marden

humor

A well-developed sense of humor is the pole that adds balance
to your steps as you walk the tightrope of life.

Jim Rohn

it's a dance

Harmony is the inner cadence of contentment we feel when the melody of life is in tune. Sarah Ban Breathnach

Happiness is when what you think, what you say, and what you do are in harmony. Mahatma Gandhi

Happiness is mental harmony; unhappiness is mental inharmony. James Allen

THINK ABOUT THAT

But what is happiness except the simple harmony between a man and the life he leads? Albert Camus

Peace is the result of retraining your mind to process life as it is, rather than as you think it should be. Wayne W. Dyer

harmony inside

You are only afraid if you are
not in harmony with yourself.
Hermann Hesse

Only by learning to live in
harmony with your
contradictions can you keep it
all afloat. Audre Lorde

If you restore balance in your
own self, you will be
contributing immensely to the
healing of the world. Deepak
Chopra

key takeaways

DO'S

 Schedule dedicated time for work, leisure, relationships, and self-care. Include buffer zones to avoid feeling rushed.

 Be okay with the present moment. Be okay with your current state. Embrace it.

 Be smart about what you let go, and what you hold on to. Some things are not worth it.

DONT'S

 Don't be "on" 100% of the time. Learn to be 100% off too. You need both.

 Don't think life has to be perfect to be wonderful. Harmony is being fine with the imperfections.

 Don't be so serious. Harmony is reached through love and humor.

part 4

serenity

You can't control what happens around you.
But you can control what goes on inside.
Focusing on the right things leads to inner peace.

40

Inner peace through serenity

THE QUIET MOMENTS

Actress <u>Emma Thompson</u> is a powerhouse on screen, but her off-screen life is all about serenity. "Nature is my sanctuary," she said in an interview. Emma finds inner peace by spending time gardening and walking in the English countryside.

"There's something about being present in nature, the sound of birds, the feel of soil," she explains.

This connection to the natural world allows Emma to quiet her mind and appreciate the simple beauty around her. It's a reminder that serenity can be found not in grand gestures, but in the quiet moments of connection with the natural world.

Her story shows that inner peace can bloom anywhere we can find a way to be present and appreciate the world around us.

This moment is fine. Naval Ravikant

Decide that wherever
you are, is the best place
there is.
Sodo Yokoyama

the beauty inside

There is a place in you that you
must keep inviolate, a place
that you must keep clean.
Maya Angelou

The person who is not
disturbed by happiness and
distress and is steady in both is
certainly eligible for liberation.
Bhagavad Gita

When completely relaxed, we
experience the essence of our
being, the deep silence that
knows everything as it is.
Haemin Sunim

it's simple

BE, ENJOY BEING
Just be, and enjoy being. Eckhart
Tolle

BODY, MIND
Movement is good for the body.
Stillness is good for the mind.
Sakyong Mipham

SIT, WATCH
Don't be afraid to just sit and
watch. Anthony Bourdain

Every breath we take, every step we make, can be filled with peace, joy and serenity. Thich Nhat Hanh

it's fine here

Harmony is the feeling that arises from not wanting
to be somewhere else, doing something else.

Raj Raghunathan

don't escape – collaborate

Our path is to collaborate with what's happening. Not to fight it.

Rick Rubin

make this trade

Serenity comes when you trade expectations for acceptance.

feel relaxed

Attachment, need, and desire all must go if one wishes to remain at peace. James Pierce

Relax and let go of any tension. Rhonda Byrne

Relax. Nothing is under control. Adi Da

When you let go of fear of the future, your soul feels light. Courtney Carver

THINK ABOUT THAT

When you are relaxed you become porous. When you are tense you are closed. Osho

My jealousy of dogs: They can sit for hours doing absolutely nothing, appearing perfectly content. Morgan Housel

the right thing

When you do the right thing,
you get the feeling of peace
and serenity associated with it.
Do it again and again. Roy T.
Bennett

Just that you do the right
thing. The rest doesn't matter.
Marcus Aurelius

Do your work, then step back.
The only path to serenity. Lao
Tzu

key takeaways

DO'S

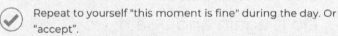 Repeat to yourself "this moment is fine" during the day. Or "accept".

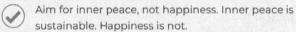 Aim for inner peace, not happiness. Inner peace is sustainable. Happiness is not.

Remember serenity is being fine with whatever happens, good or bad, and then acting without expectations.

DONT'S

 Don't be tense. Just be focused on the task at hand.

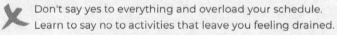 Don't say yes to everything and overload your schedule. Learn to say no to activities that leave you feeling drained.

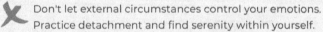 Don't let external circumstances control your emotions. Practice detachment and find serenity within yourself.

part 5

zen

Learn about Zen. Learn to contemplate, observe,
and reflect. Learn to be more meditative.
Learn to remove before adding.

Inner peace through Zen practice

THE PROCESS VS THE OUTCOME

Eugen Herrigel was a German philosopher who traveled to Japan to learn archery under a Zen master. He envisioned mastering the art with perfect form and impressive bullseye.

However, the master focused on something different. For months, Herrigel just practiced drawing the bow without ever firing an arrow. Frustrated, he demanded to learn the actual shooting.

The master smiled and said, "You are not ready. You are too focused on the result, on hitting the target. Archery is about the present moment, the breath, the feeling of the bow."

Finally, after months of this seemingly pointless exercise, Herrigel understood. He wasn't just learning archery; he was learning Zen. He learned to let go of his obsession with the outcome and focus on the present moment, the feeling of the bow becoming an extension of himself.

One day, the master silently told Herrigel to shoot. Herrigel released the arrow, and to his surprise, it hit the bullseye. He realized Zen archery wasn't about hitting the target; it was about the journey, the focus, and the inner peace that came from being present in the moment.

The beauty of Zen is found in simplicity and tranquility, in a sense of the all-embracing harmony of things.
Thich Thien-An

embrace reality

I live by letting things happen.
Dogen

Let go, or be dragged. Zen
proverb

One loses joy and happiness in
the attempt to possess them.
Masanobu Fukuoka

Only the hand that
erases can write the true
thing. Meister Eckhart

patience

THE MUD
Do you have the patience to wait until your mud settles and the water is clear? Lao Tzu

NO THOUGHTS
When thoughts arise, then do all things arise. When thoughts vanish, then do all things vanish. Huang Po

BE 100% HERE
Still your waters. Josh Waitzkin

Zen practice is
to open up our
small mind.
Shunryu Suzuki

become aware

Zen teaches nothing; it merely enables us
to wake up and become aware.
It does not teach, it points.

D.T. Suzuki

from bondage
to freedom

Zen in it's essence is the art of seeing into
the nature of one's being, and it points
the way from bondage to freedom.

D.T. Suzuki

only this moment

Zen is a liberation from time.
For if we open our eyes and see clearly,
it becomes obvious that there is no other time than this instant,
and that the past and the future are abstractions
without any concrete reality.

Alan Watts

here and now

Zen is not some kind of excitement, but concentration on our usual everyday routine. Shunryu Suzuki

Treat every moment as your last. It is not preparation for something else. Shunryu Suzuki

The noble-minded are calm and steady. Little people are forever fussing and fretting. Confucius

total presence

Do not dwell in the past, do not dream of the future, concentrate the mind on the present moment. Buddha

I follow four dictates: face it, accept it, deal with it, then let it go. Sheng-yen

Be present above all else. Naval Ravikant

key takeaways

DO'S

 Keep things simple and give 100% of your attention to *one* thing.

 Practice non-attachment to material possessions, desires, or outcomes. Appreciate things without clinging to them.

 Be more patient and do things more slowly. There's no rush.

DONT'S

 Don't fill your mind with junk news and your spare with with junk activities.

 Don't multitask. You're losing time, efficacy, and energy.

 Don't live your life carelessly. Be here, now, in the moment.

part 6

gratitude & contentment

Discover why gratitude is the path to happiness.
Learn how to be content with less.
Learn what's being "rich".

Inner peace through gratitude

THE AIR, THE WATER — IT'S A GIFT

Astronaut <u>Ron Garan</u> spent 177 days living on the International Space Station. While orbiting Earth, he saw our planet from a whole new perspective. It was a breathtaking sight, a fragile blue marble suspended in the vast blackness of space.

The experience filled Garan with immense gratitude. He took pictures every day, focusing on Earth's beauty and the preciousness of our home.

Back on Earth, people asked him about the wonders of space. Garan would smile and say, "It's not just about space, it's about how it makes you appreciate Earth. The air you breathe, the water you drink, all this...it's a gift."

Garan's story shows how gratitude can blossom from a shift in perspective. Sometimes, a little distance can help you appreciate what you often take for granted. By taking a moment to be grateful for the ordinary miracles around you, you can cultivate a sense of peace and wonder in your everyday life.

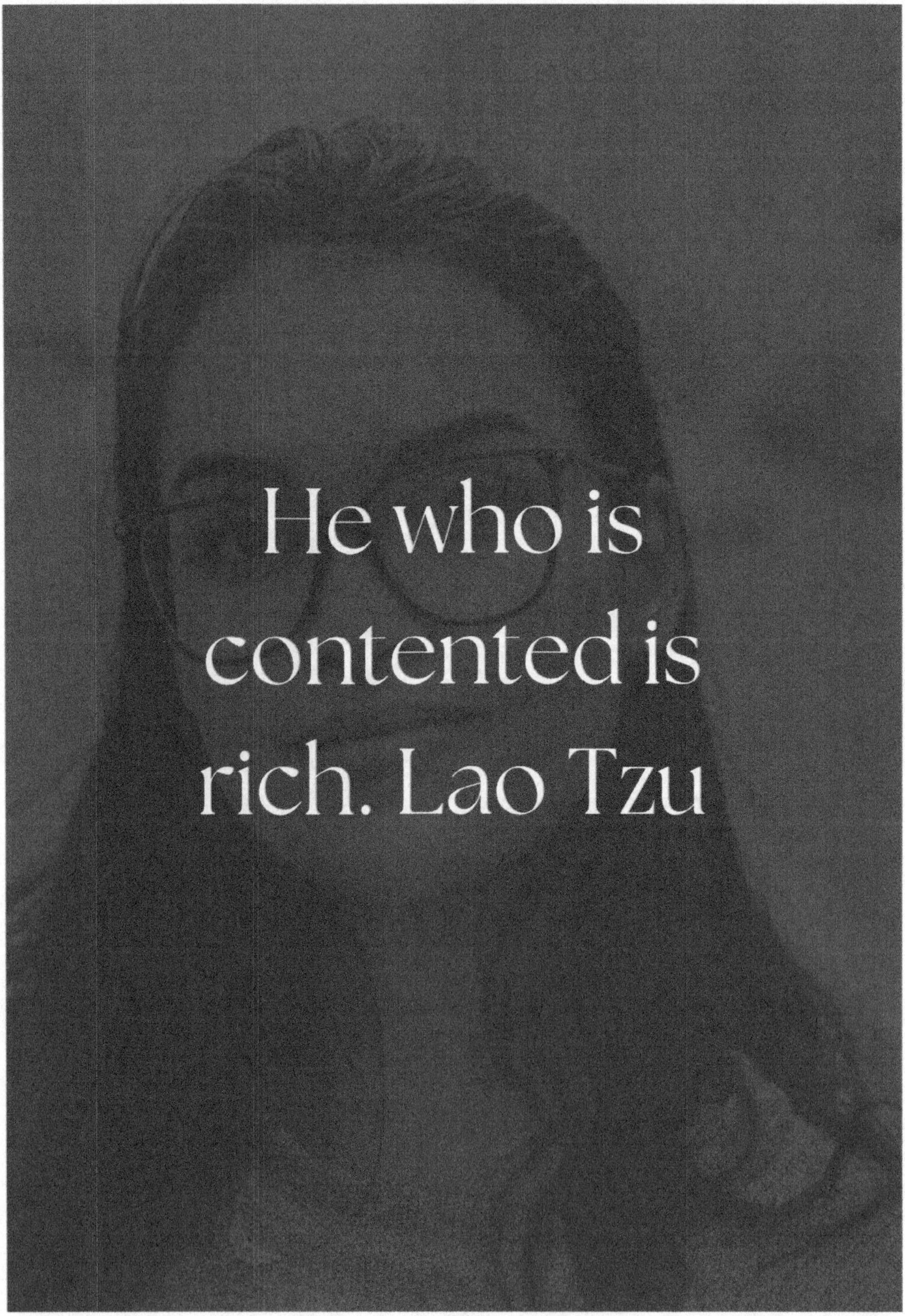

He who is
contented is
rich. Lao Tzu

you are rich

Gratitude turns what we have into enough. Aesop

Gratitude is riches. Complaint is poverty. Doris Day

If the only prayer you said in your whole life was "thank you" that would suffice. Meister Eckhart

This is a wonderful day.
I've never seen this one
before. Maya Angelou

be grateful

YOU'RE LUCKY
The world gives you way more than you ever give it. Kamal Ravikant

YOU'RE FORTUNATE
So much has been given to me; I have no time to ponder over that which has been denied. Helen Keller (Helen Keller was blind)

YOU'RE BLESSED
If a fellow isn't thankful for what he's got, he isn't likely to be thankful for what he's going to get. Frank A. Clark

As long as this exists, this sunshine and this cloudless sky, and as long as I can enjoy it, how can I be sad?
Anne Frank

you have enough

Gratitude is what you feel when you want
what you already have.

James Clear

"now" is fine

True happiness is to enjoy the present,
without anxious dependence upon the
future, not to amuse ourselves with
either hopes or fears but to rest satisfied
with what we have, which is sufficient,
for he that is so wants nothing.

Seneca

be happy with less

Contentment, as it is a short road and pleasant,
has great delight and little trouble.

Epictetus

abundance

Giving thanks for abundance is greater than the abundance itself. Rumi

The best way to pay for a lovely moment is to enjoy it. Richard Bach

There are always flowers for those who want to see them. Henri Matisse

Stop now. Enjoy the moment. It's now, or never. Maxime Lagacé

THINK ABOUT THAT

I was complaining that I had no shoes till I met a man who had no feet. Confucius

We can complain because rose bushes have thorns, or rejoice because thorns have roses. Alphonse Karr

Don't cry because it's over, smile because it happened. Dr. Seuss

the ordinary
is extraordinary

Gratitude can transform common days into thanksgivings, turn routine jobs into joy, and change ordinary opportunities into blessings. William Arthur Ward

He is a wise man who does not grieve for the things which he has not, but rejoices for those which he has. Epictetus

He who is not contented with what he has, would not be contented with what he would like to have. Socrates

key takeaways

DO'S

 Desire less. Be content with less. Be free.

 Learn to see each day as a gift, a miracle, because it is.

 Start a gratitude journal. Spend 5-10 minutes each day writing down 3-5 things you're grateful for, big or small.

DONT'S

 Don't take anything for granted. Anything you have could be gone tomorrow.

 Don't complain. Learn to stay peaceful no matter what.

 Don't seek the extraordinary. Remember you don't need much to be happy.

part 7

happiness

With wisdom and inner peace,
you're on the fast track to happiness.

Inner peace by being you, happy, imperfect

HUMAN, AND FLAWED

Actress <u>Emma Watson</u>, known for her role as Hermione Granger, found inner peace by letting go of perfectionism. "I used to be really hard on myself," she said. "But happiness isn't about being perfect, it's about embracing your flaws."

Today, Emma focuses on self-compassion and enjoying the journey. She reads for pleasure, takes long walks, and prioritizes activities that bring her joy, not stress. "It's about feeling good in my own skin," she explains.

By letting go of unrealistic expectations, Emma found inner peace and discovered that happiness comes from simply being herself.

This shift reminds you that true happiness lies in self-acceptance, not chasing an impossible ideal.

80

Happiness is a
state where
nothing is
missing. Naval
Ravikant

right here, right now

True happiness arises, in the
first place, from the enjoyment
of one's self. Joseph Addison

Stop trying so hard to reach
happiness. Simply accept the
moment as it is. Maxime
Lagacé

Happiness, not in another
place but this place...not for
another hour, but this hour.
Walt Whitman

Now and then it's good
to pause in our pursuit of
happiness and just be
happy. Guillaume
Apollinaire

happiness is a mindset

YOU'RE RESPONSIBLE
Happiness depends upon ourselves.
Aristotle

YOU'RE IN CONTROL OF YOURSELF
Life is 10 percent what happens to
you and 90 percent how you
respond to it. Lou Holtz

YOU'RE CALM AND CONFIDENT
Be a lamp for yourselves. Be your
own refuge. Buddha

Happiness comes from peace. Peace comes from indifference. Naval Ravikant

relax

Tension is who you think you should be,
relaxation is who you are.

Chinese proverb

don't take it seriously

It is more fitting for a man to laugh at life than to lament over it.

Seneca

happiness is within

Happiness can only be found within, by breaking attachments
to external things and cultivating an attitude of acceptance.

Jonathan Haidt

imperfect is perfect

Today might not be perfect, but it's a perfect day to be happy. Lori Deschene

A beautiful thing is never perfect. Egyptian proverb

We never taste happiness in perfection, our most fortunate successes are mixed with sadness. Pierre Corneille

THINK ABOUT THAT

Life does not have to be perfect to be wonderful. Annette Funicello

To be in harmony with the wholeness of things is not to have anxiety over imperfections. Dogen

only when you stop

Happiness is a gift and the trick is not to expect it, but to delight in it when it comes. Charles Dickens

It's ironic that the thing that will bring you happiness is giving up the search for happiness. Naval Ravikant

You can only have bliss if you don't chase it. Henepola Gunaratana

key takeaways

DO'S

 Just pause. Right now. Stop seeking. Enjoy *this* moment.

 Do something creative for 30 minutes, even if it's just coloring or doodling. Creativity can be a form of self-expression, relaxation, and liberation.

 Remember permanent happiness doesn't exist. Be fine with it.

DONT'S

 Don't postpone happiness. You'll never arrive at it. Be satisfied with less.

 Don't confuse happiness with material possessions. Studies show that experiences and relationships bring more lasting happiness than material things.

 Don't try to be the general manager of the universe. Don't be a control freak. Let go.

part 8

stoicism

Discover stoicism: a way of life and a practical philosophy to help you find peace no matter the circumstances.

92

Inner peace through stoicism

JUST GIVE YOUR BEST

Tennis champion <u>Novak Djokovic</u> is known for his mental toughness on the court. But his calm demeanor comes from a surprising source: <u>stoicism</u>.

"Stoicism teaches you to accept what you cannot control and focus on what you can," Novak said.

Before big matches, Novak practices mindfulness meditation, a technique stoics used for centuries. This helps him stay present and manage his emotions. "It's not about winning or losing," he explains, "it's about giving my best effort and finding peace in the process."

Novak's stoic approach helps him stay focused and avoid getting overwhelmed by pressure, leading to inner peace and consistent success on the court.

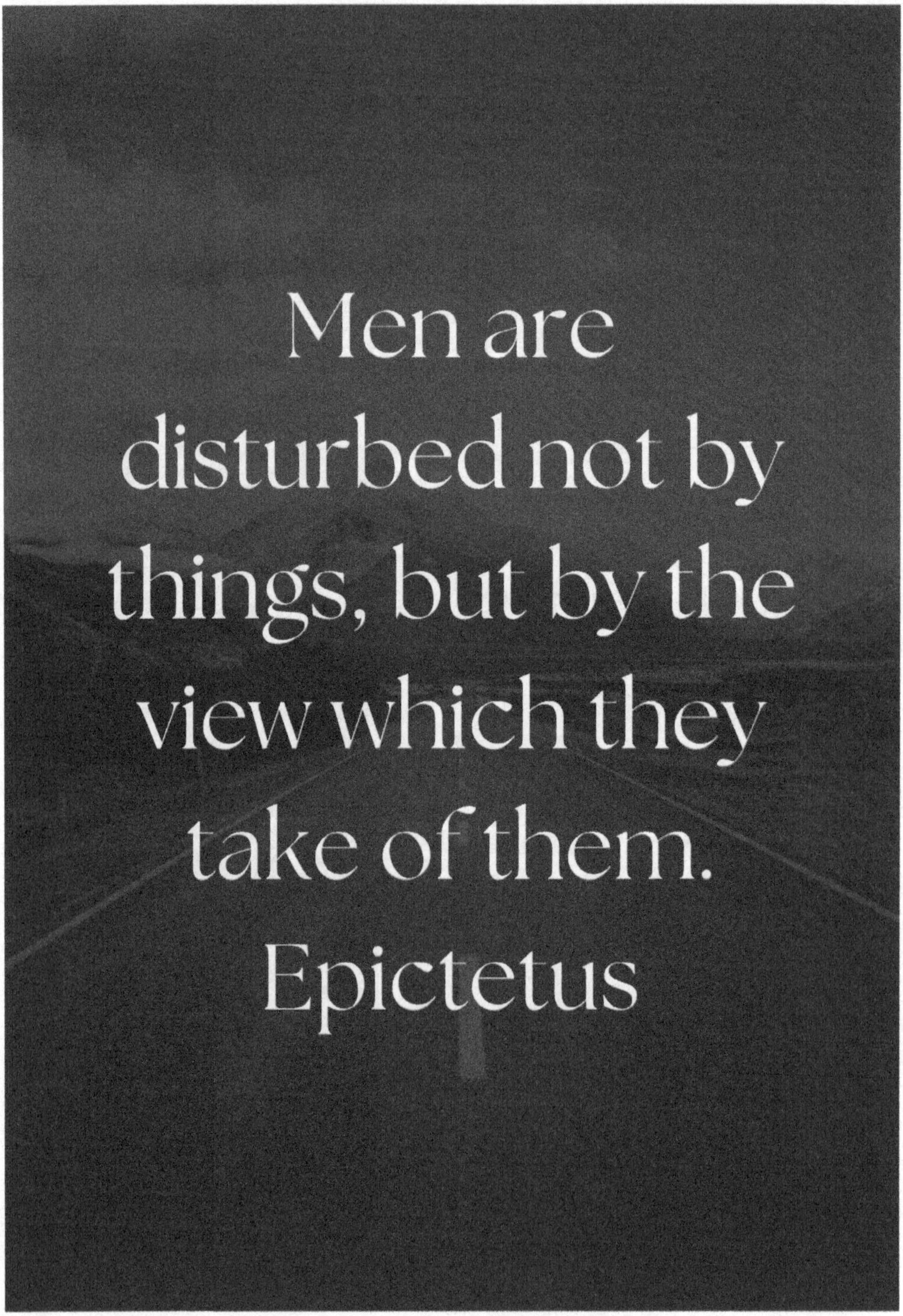

Men are
disturbed not by
things, but by the
view which they
take of them.
Epictetus

accept adversity

A gem cannot be polished
without friction, nor a man
perfected without trials.
Seneca

You have power over your
mind — not outside events.
Realize this, and you will find
strength. Marcus Aurelius

Winter, summer, happiness,
and pain; Giving, appearing,
disappearing; Non-permanent,
all of them; Just try to tolerate.
Bhagavad Gita

What is to give light must
endure burning. Viktor Frankl

Learn to be
indifferent to what
makes no difference.
Marcus Aurelius

what is stoicism?

BE CALM

To be stoic is not to be emotionless, but to remain unaffected by your emotions. James Pierce

DON'T COMPLAIN

To complain is always nonacceptance of what is. Eckhart Tolle

BE PATIENT

Doing what's right sometimes requires patience. Marcus Aurelius

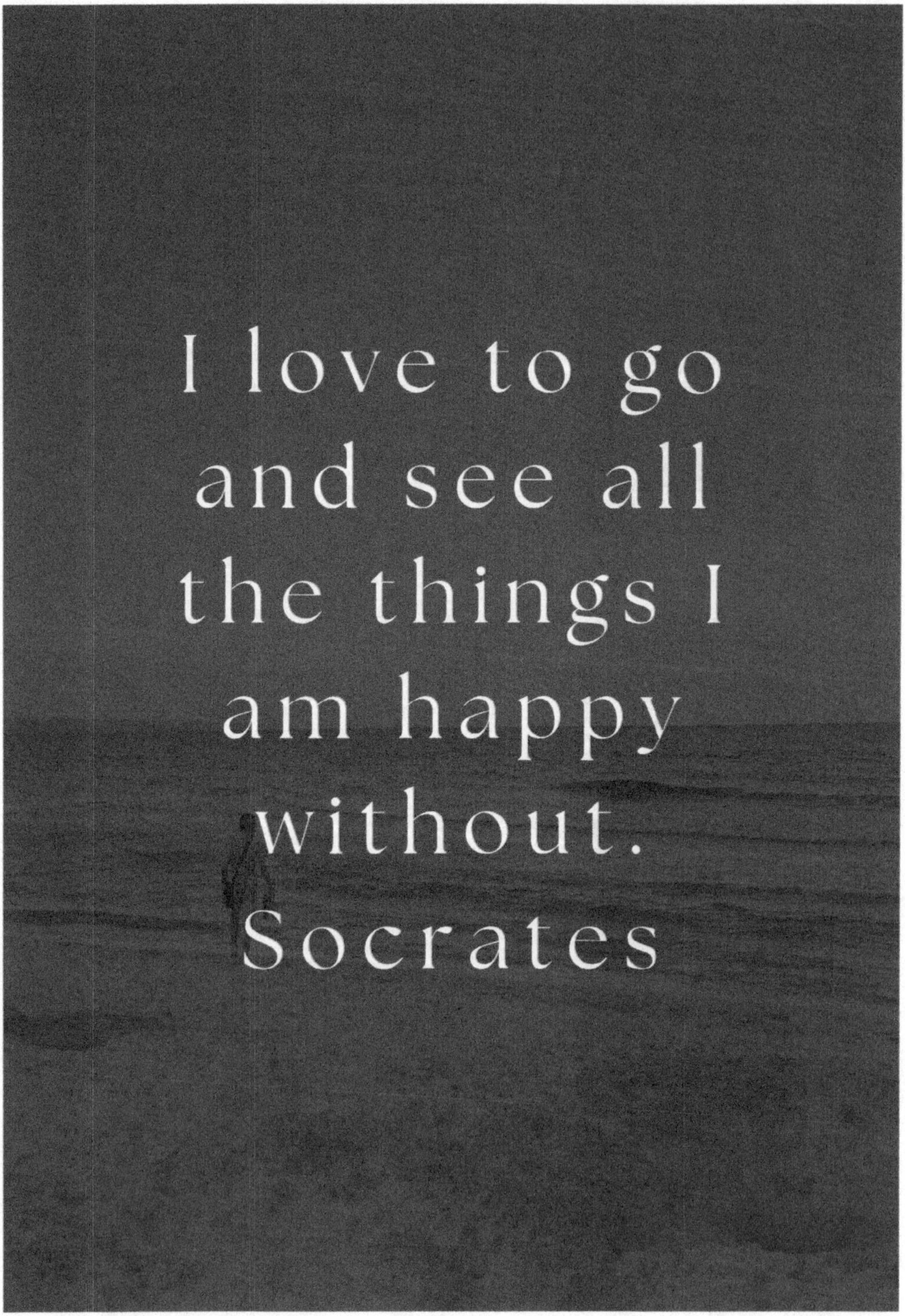

I love to go
and see all
the things I
am happy
without.
Socrates

it's all natural

Treat whatever happens as wholly natural;
not novel or hard to deal with;
but familiar and easily handled.

Marcus Aurelius

value your time

Relentlessly prune bullshit, don't wait
to do things that matter,
and savor the time you have.

Paul Graham

life is hard (and it's fine)

If you are irritated by every rub,
how will your mirror be polished?

Rumi

don't be so serious

It does not matter what you bear, but how you bear it. Seneca

The robbed that smiles steals something from the thief. Othello

Life is a shipwreck, but we must not forget to sing in the lifeboats. Voltaire

I love those who can smile in trouble. Leonardo da Vinci

THINK ABOUT THAT

Very little is needed to make a happy life; it is all within yourself, in your way of thinking. Marcus Aurelius

The cucumber is bitter? Then throw it out. There are brambles in the path? Then go around them. Marcus Aurelius

accept your fate

Fate leads the willing, and
drags along the reluctant.
Seneca

That one wants nothing to be
different, not forward, not
backwards, not in all eternity.
Not merely bear what is
necessary, still less conceal it...
but love it. Friedrich Nietzsche

Willingly accept what's outside
your control. Ryan Holiday

key takeaways

DO'S

 Remain unaffected when things go wrong. See everything as natural.

 Develop a mindful approach to desires. Don't be ruled by fleeting pleasures.

 Embrace adversity. Without it, you would remain weak.

DONT'S

 Don't avoid responsibility. You're not a victim. You're in charge.

 Don't let your happiness depend on external factors like praise, approval, or material possessions.

 Don't hang on to anger and sadness. Acknowledge these emotions, but don't let them control you.

part 9

simplicity & minimalism

Inner peace is easier when you simplify your life and reject materialism as a way of life. Keep in mind: only a handful of things are vital. Do you know them?

Inner peace through simplicity

A SMALL CABIN

Once upon a time, there was a guy named Henry David Thoreau. He was all about simplifying life. One day, he packed his bags and headed into the woods near Walden Pond (USA), aiming to live with just the basics. No fancy stuff, no frills.

Thoreau wasn't into the whole rat race thing. He wanted peace, simplicity, and connection with nature. So, he built himself a tiny cabin and lived there for two years.

During his time in the woods, Thoreau discovered something profound. With fewer possessions and distractions, he found more meaning. He didn't need all that excess stuff to be happy. Just the simple joys of nature and self-reflection.

In sum, Thoreau's experiment teaches a valuable lesson: less stuff leads to more inner peace. And it's not about what you own; it's about what you experience and cherish.

Simplicity boils down to two steps: Identify the essential. Eliminate the rest. Leo Babauta

become free

The more you have, the more you are occupied. The less you have, the more free you are. Mother Teresa

Things that matter most must never be at the mercy of things that matter least. Johann Wolfgang von Goethe

Make room for things that matter by removing everything that doesn't. Brian Gardner

Saying no is more important than saying yes. Shane Parrish

less

WANT LESS
My greatest skill has been to want little. Henry David Thoreau

KEEP IT SIMPLE
Manifest plainness, embrace simplicity, reduce selfishness, have few desires. Lao Tzu

KNOW WHAT'S IMPORTANT
Discern the vital few from the trivial many. Greg McKeown

Too many people spend money they haven't earned to buy things they don't want to impress people they don't like. Will Rogers

ignore things

The art of being wise is the art of knowing
what to overlook.

William James

be selective

Being overwhelmed is often as
unproductive as doing nothing, and
is far more unpleasant. Being
selective – doing less – is the path of
the productive.

Tim Ferriss

the simple life

Possessions, outward success, publicity, luxury – to me these have always been contemptible. I believe that a simple and unassuming manner of life is best for everyone, best for both the body and the mind.

Albert Einstein

desire, but less

To be richer, happier, and freer, all you need to do is want less. Francine Jay

The greatest wealth is a poverty of desires. Seneca

Order your soul. Reduce your wants. Augustine of Hippo

If I'm not saying 'Hell Yeah!' to something, then I say no. Derek Sivers

THINK ABOUT THAT

Every increased possession loads us with new weariness. John Ruskin

How trivial the things we want so passionately are. Marcus Aurelius

If buying stuff hasn't made you happy, maybe getting rid of it will. Joshua Becker

value the right things

If everything is important, then nothing is. Patrick M. Lencioni

Getting rid of everything that doesn't matter allows you to remember who you are. Courtney Carver

Almost everything is noise, and a very few things are exceptionally valuable. Greg McKeown

key takeaways

DO'S

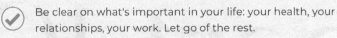 Be clear on what's important in your life: your health, your relationships, your work. Let go of the rest.

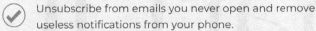 Unsubscribe from emails you never open and remove useless notifications from your phone.

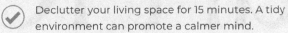 Declutter your living space for 15 minutes. A tidy environment can promote a calmer mind.

DONT'S

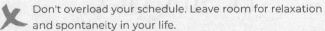 Don't overload your schedule. Leave room for relaxation and spontaneity in your life.

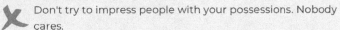 Don't try to impress people with your possessions. Nobody cares.

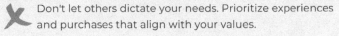 Don't let others dictate your needs. Prioritize experiences and purchases that align with your values.

part 10

resilience

Inner peace is about letting go, but it's also about
living for your values and what you believe in.

Inner peace through resilience

JUST GET UP AND KEEP GOING

Actor <u>Tom Hanks</u> is known for his friendly demeanor, but his path wasn't always easy.

Early in his career, he faced rejection after rejection. "There were a lot of 'no's,'" he said. "But you can't let those define you."

Tom persevered, focusing on his craft and staying positive. He built strong relationships with other actors and found joy in the process, not just the outcome. "It's not about winning. It's about getting up after you lose."

This resilience and focus on the journey eventually led him to become one of Hollywood's most respected actors.

Tom's story reminds you that inner peace can come from accepting setbacks and celebrating the climb, all while cherishing the connections you make along the way.

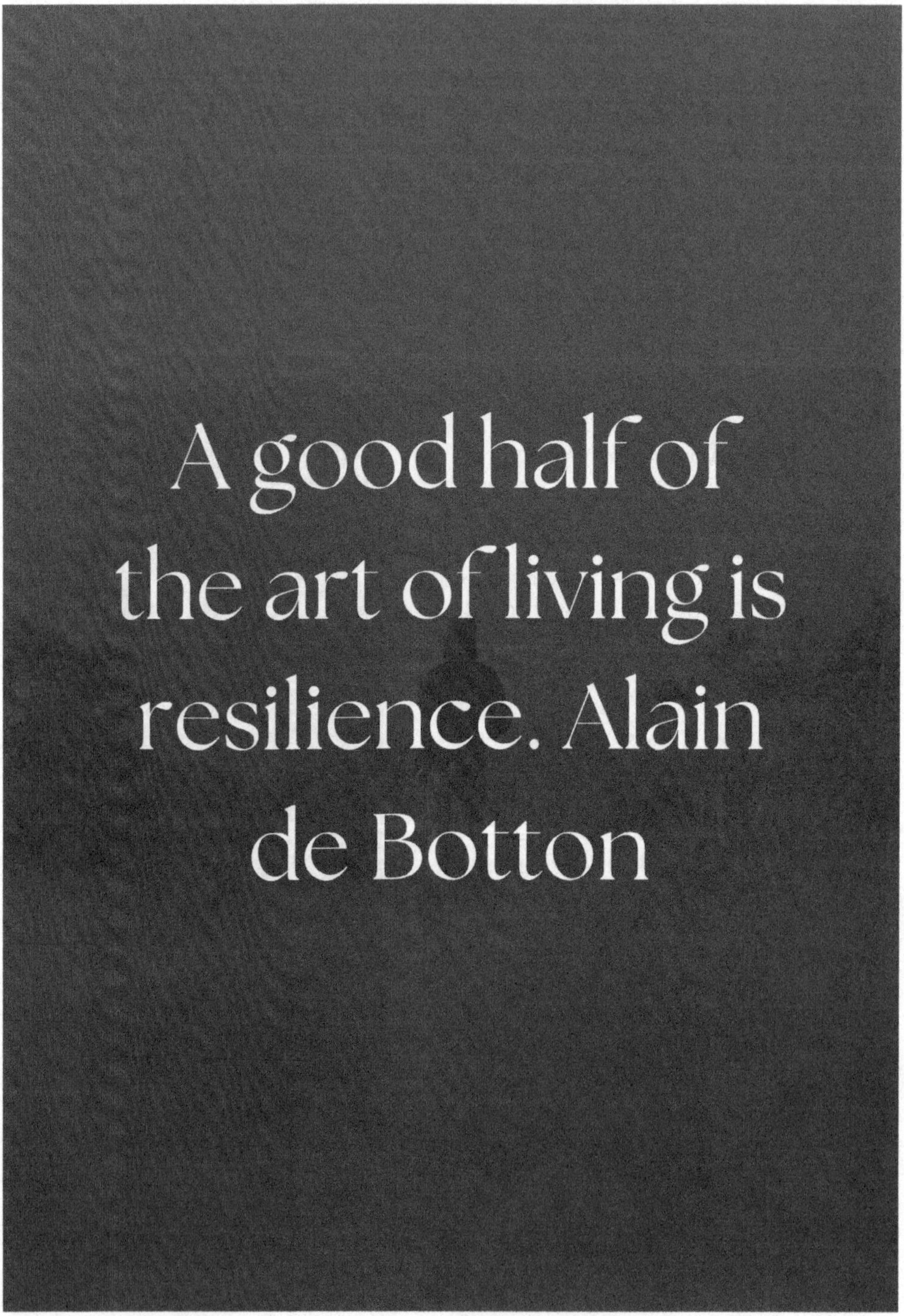

A good half of
the art of living is
resilience. Alain
de Botton

adversity is useful

You need patience, discipline,
and agility to take losses and
adversity without going crazy.
Charlie Munger

Suffering is part of our training
program for becoming wise.
Ram Dass

Make the mind tougher by
exposing it to adversity. Robert
Greene

If you're overwhelmed
by the size of a problem,
break it down into
smaller pieces. Chuck
Close

keep going, patiently

OBSTACLES ARE NEEDED
In general, obstacles force your mind to focus and find ways around them. They heighten your mental powers and should be welcomed. Robert Greene

DARKNESS IS NEEDED
Only in the darkness can you see the stars. Martin Luther King Jr

GRAPES NEED TIME
Nothing important comes into being overnight; even grapes and figs need time to ripen. Epictetus

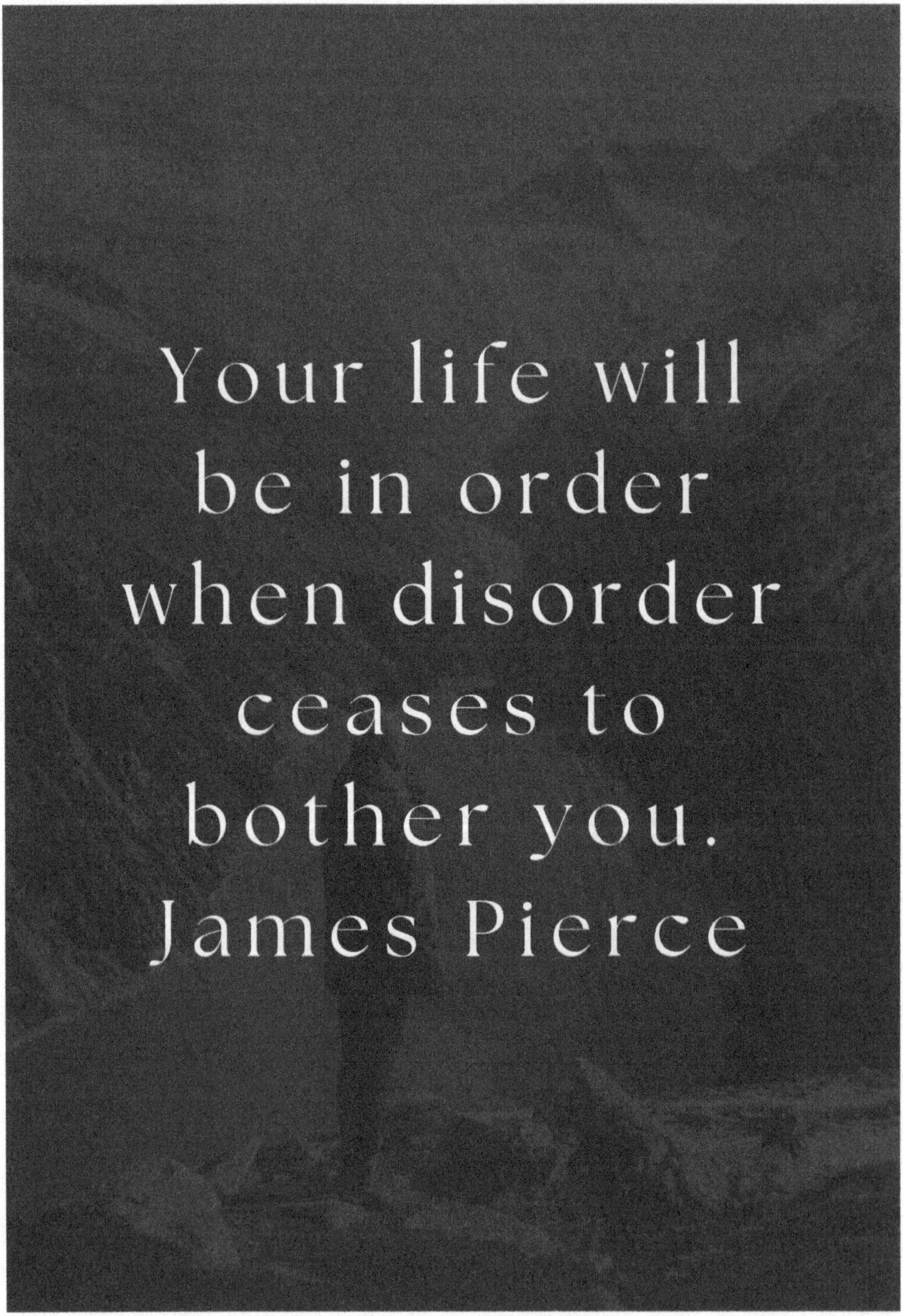

Your life will
be in order
when disorder
ceases to
bother you.
James Pierce

it's your perspective

It's not the problem that causes our suffering;
it's our thinking about the problem.

Byron Katie

discomfort is fine

Relax.
You're not supposed
to be happy all the time.

Maxime Lagacé

keep swimming

Sometimes the tide is with us, and sometimes against.
But we keep swimming either way.

Charlie Munger

no challenge,
no satisfaction

Inner peace is not minding that it hurts. Maxime Lagacé

Stop looking for a sign that the hard time will end. David Goggins

People need hard times and oppression to develop psychic muscles. Emily Dickinson

THINK ABOUT THAT

There were good times, there were hard times, but there were never bad times. Steve Jobs

Hard times produce your greatest gifts. Robin Sharma

What if solving worthwhile problems is how we enjoy life? Naval Ravikant

water is there

Dark times are not hopeless
times. David Goggins

Nothing in life is to be feared, it
is only to be understood. Marie
Curie

Work. Keep digging your well.
Water is there somewhere.
Rumi

key takeaways

DO'S

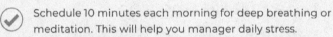 Schedule 10 minutes each morning for deep breathing or meditation. This will help you manager daily stress.

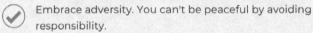 Embrace adversity. You can't be peaceful by avoiding responsibility.

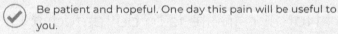 Be patient and hopeful. One day this pain will be useful to you.

DONT'S

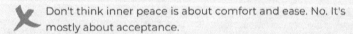 Don't think inner peace is about comfort and ease. No. It's mostly about acceptance.

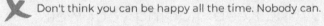 Don't think you can be happy all the time. Nobody can.

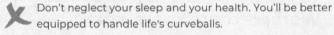 Don't neglect your sleep and your health. You'll be better equipped to handle life's curveballs.

part 11

relationships

It's hard to be peaceful when you have toxic
relationships. Leave those behind.
Spend more time with the right ones.

Inner peace through relationships

THE COMMUNITY, THE SUPPORT

Singer Alicia Keys has a successful career, but her true sense of peace comes from community.

She grew up in a tight-knit neighborhood in New York City. "We were all like family," she says. "There was this inherent sense of 'we're in this together.'"

Even now, Alicia surrounds herself with supportive friends and family. She also spends time volunteering in her community. "It's a constant reminder that we're all connected".

This connection to others helps her stay grounded and keeps things in perspective. Alicia feels her purpose extends beyond the stage, and that brings her a deep sense of happiness and inner peace.

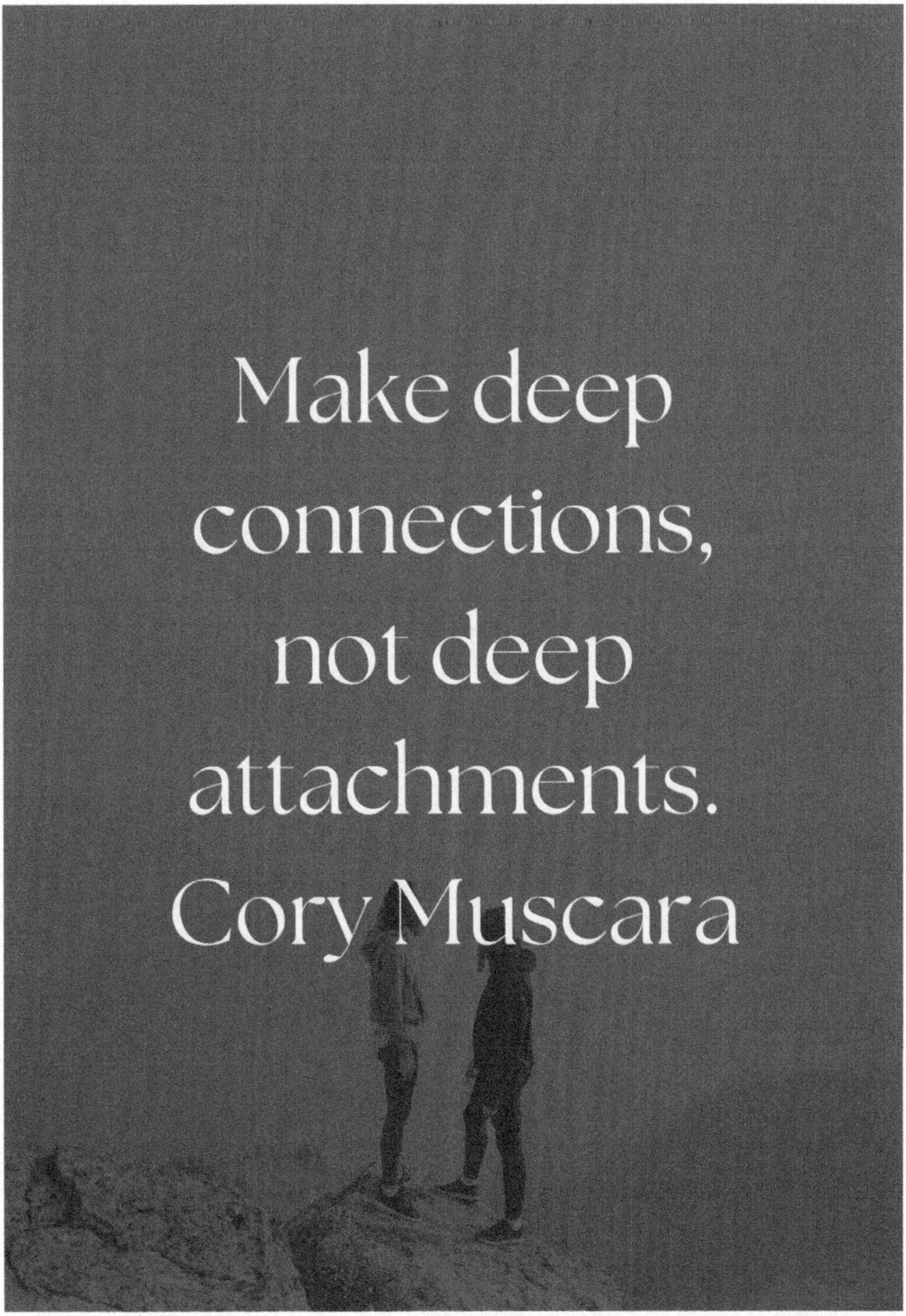

Make deep
connections,
not deep
attachments.
Cory Muscara

your tribe

Life is nothing without
friendship. Cicero

Surround yourself with those
who only lift you higher. Oprah
Winfrey

You become like the five
people you spend the most
time with. Choose carefully.
Jim Rohn

Your relationship with others is a direct reflection of your relationship with yourself. Mark Manson

be well surrounded

THIS IS TOXIC
Stay away from negative people. They have a problem for every solution. Albert Einstein

THIS IS THE KEY
The key is to keep company only with people who uplift you, whose presence calls forth your best. Epictetus

THIS IS ENOUGH
I have learned that to be with those I like is enough. Walt Whitman

Less time
scrolling,
more time
connecting.

forgive others

Forgive others, not because they deserve it,
but because you deserve inner peace.

Sai Baba

precious time

There's only one thing more precious
than our time and that's who we
spend it on.

Leo Christopher

serve people

The sole meaning of life is to serve humanity.

Leo Tolstoy

140

be a rainbow

Try to be a rainbow in someone's cloud. Maya Angelou

How far that little candle throws his beams! So shines a good deed in a weary world. William Shakespeare

Kindness is the sunshine in which virtue grows. Robert Green Ingersoll

A single sunbeam is enough to drive away many shadows. Francis of Assisi

THINK ABOUT THAT

Kindness and empathy is not weakness, it's strength. Lex Fridman

What wisdom can you find that is greater than kindness? Jean-Jacques Rousseau

care for others

So much of life is being
present with the people you
love. Shane Parrish

When our friends are present,
we ought to treat them well;
and when they are absent, to
speak of them well. Epictetus

We rise by lifting others.
Robert Ingersoll

key takeaways

DO'S

 Remember the happiest people are the ones with close relationships (See <u>Harvard happiness study</u>)

 Write down 2-3 persons you love spending time with. And spend some time with one of them today, or tomorrow.

 Use the 2 keys to great relationships: acceptance and generosity.

DONT'S

 Don't isolate. Some solitude is fine, but feeling lonely is not.

 Don't hang with toxic people (people who gossip, complain, discourage, etc.)

 Don't be the *taker* in your relationships. Be the *giver*.

part 12

physical &
mental health

Inner peace follows mental health,
which follows physical health.

Inner peace through health

A HEALTHY BODY BODY AND MIND

Consider the journey of Dwayne "The Rock" Johnson, the renowned actor and former professional wrestler. Despite his busy schedule and demanding career, Johnson prioritizes both his physical and mental health as essential components of inner peace and happiness.

Johnson openly shares his struggles with mental health challenges, including depression and anxiety, which he faced during his early adulthood. Recognizing the importance of seeking help and taking care of his mental well-being, Johnson sought therapy and developed coping strategies to manage his mental health.

In addition to his focus on mental health, Johnson also emphasizes the importance of physical fitness in maintaining inner peace. He follows a disciplined workout routine and prioritizes healthy eating habits to keep his body strong and energized.

Through his journey, Johnson inspires others to prioritize both their physical and mental health, showing that true inner peace and happiness come from nurturing both aspects of well-being.

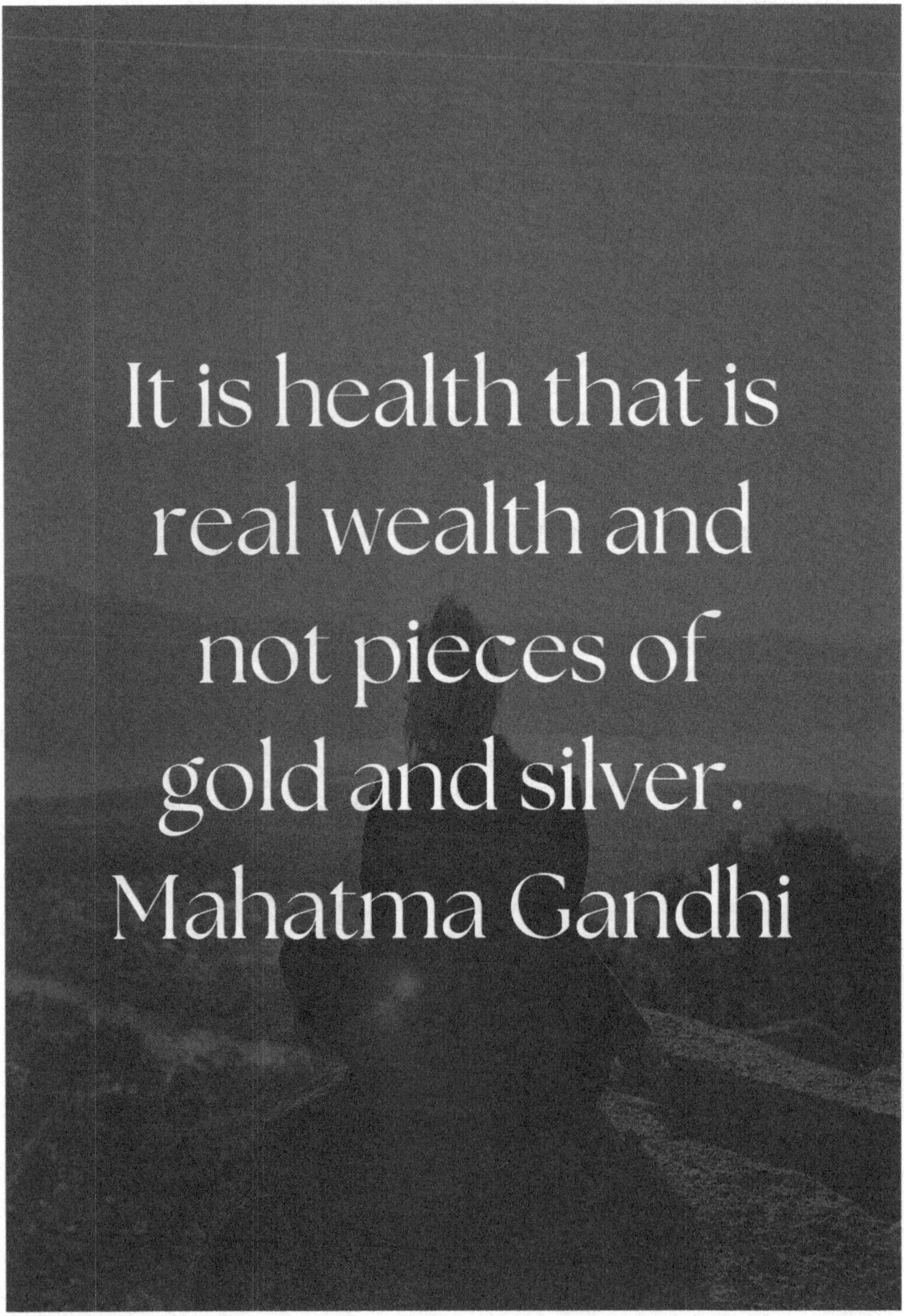

It is health that is
real wealth and
not pieces of
gold and silver.
Mahatma Gandhi

health is everything

He who has health has hope;
and he who has hope has
everything. Arabian proverb

What is called genius is the
abundance of life and health.
Henry David Thoreau

The greatest of follies is to
sacrifice health for any other
kind of happiness. Arthur
Schopenhauer

People feel tired
but sit for 12 hours.

People feel overwhelmed
but look at their phone for 2+ hours.

People feel depressed
but spend most of their time inside.

A lesson.

148

take care of yourself

LAUGH, SLEEP
A good laugh and a long sleep are the best cures in the doctor's book. Irish proverb

EXERCISE
It is exercise alone that supports the spirits, and keeps the mind in vigor. Marcus Tullius Cicero

STAY ACTIVE
Feeling physically and mentally well is our own individual obligation. Andrew Huberman

Keep your vitality. A life without health is like a river without water. Maxime Lagacé

an ancient balance

The modern mind is overstimulated and the modern body is understimulated and overfed. Meditation, exercise, and fasting restore an ancient balance.

Naval Ravikant

take responsibility

Doctors won't make you healthy.
Nutritionists won't make you slim.
Teachers won't make you smart.
Gurus won't make you calm.
Mentors won't make you rich.
Trainers won't make you fit.
Ultimately, you have to take responsibility.
Save yourself.

Naval Ravikant

three things

To feel better, do three things: diet, exercise and sleep.

Justin Kan

body & mind

Take care of your body. It's the only place you have to live. Jim Rohn

Let your body be your holy temple. Lailah Gifty Akita

The highest level of mental health cannot be achieved without a high level of physical health. Train both. Gal Shapira

exercise

The biggest benefit of exercise isn't your physical health, it's your mental health. Matthew Kobach

The ultimate list of biohacks and smart drugs: Drink more water, get 8 hours of sleep, walk outside in the sun, leave your phone on silent, read a few pages each day, eat more vegetables and greens, don't hang out with toxic people, work on projects you care about. James Clear

Walking is the best possible exercise. Habituate yourself to walk very far. Thomas Jefferson

key takeaways

DO'S

 Remember inner peace starts with your health. No health, no peace. **Make it your #1 priority.**

 Spend at least 30 minutes outside every day. Walk, bike, run, hike in nature. Anything that makes you move.

 Have regular quality sleep. 7-9 hours. Dark and cold room. No electronics 1 hour before. Same routine every day.

DONT'S

 Don't take shortcuts. There are no hacks for health. Stick to the basics. 1. Move *daily*. 2. Rest *daily*. 3. Eat well *daily*.

 Don't become a slave to your phone. Create tech-free zones in your home, like your bedroom and dinner table.

 Don't think you can have mental health if you don't have physical health, and vice versa.

part 13

self-care & self-love

Becoming your top priority is key
to living a peaceful life.

Inner peace through self-care

MORE "ME TIME"

Beyoncé, the queen of pop herself, wasn't immune to feeling overwhelmed. Running a music empire, raising twins, constantly on the go - it took a toll. Sleepless nights, unhealthy eating, and a nagging feeling of burnout became her reality.

One day, she hit a wall. Exhausted and stressed, she knew something had to change. She started prioritizing self-care. Healthy meals, regular workouts, and most importantly, enough sleep. It wasn't selfish, it was essential.

Slowly, the change rippled outwards. Beyoncé felt more energized, her creativity soared, and her performances became even more electrifying. Inner peace wasn't about bubble baths and face masks (although those helped too). It was about putting her own well-being first, so she could truly shine.

She learned that true happiness comes from taking care of yourself first, before taking care of others.

Honor yourself by not criticizing, judging, or denying what you feel. Iyanla Vanzant

ignore opinions

Your opinion of you is the only thing that matters. Gal Shapira

The greatest thing you can give yourself is freedom from what others think. Abraham Hicks

To be comfortable in your own skin is priceless. Brian Norgard

Closing your eyes and listening to silence is self-care. Maxime Lagacé

self-care is...

BE PRIVATE
Being private, staying low-key and not telling everyone everything is self-care.

BE COMPASSIONATE
Sometimes self-care is just telling yourself that you can always try again tomorrow.

BE PATIENT
Growing at your own pace is self-care.

You alone are enough. You have nothing to prove to anyone. Maya Angelou

build your life

True self-care is not salt baths and chocolate cake,
it is making the choice to build a life you don't need
to regularly escape from.

Brianna Wiest

"you" needs you

Go back and take care of yourself.
Your body needs you, your feelings
need you, your perceptions need you.

Thich Nhat Hanh

the 6 pillars

Take care of yourself and take care of others. Daily investment in the 6 pillars
is the way: morning sunlight, daily movement, quality nutrition, stress
control, healthy relationships, deep sleep. Re-up every 24hrs so you can
contribute and support others consistently too.

Andrew Huberman

166

be your first priority

As you get wiser, you stop caring about everything and everyone. Maxime Lagacé

You are not responsible for fixing everything that is broken. You do not have to try and make everyone happy. Remember to take time for you, time to replenish. Jim Kwik

The truest way to decline is just to say, "it doesn't feel right to me." No explanation is necessary. Naval Ravikant

THINK ABOUT THAT

Everyone is not your assignment. That's why you're drained. Wesley Snipes

Be ok with not being liked. Gal Shapira

Do your thing and don't care if they like it. Tina Fey

say no, go slow

Self-care is honoring your right
to say no to doing more than
what you feel is right for you.
Yung Pueblo

The ego wants to go fast. The
soul needs to go slow. Maxime
Lagacé

Deciding what not to do is as
important as deciding what to
do. Steve Jobs

If I loved myself, truly and
deeply, what would I do?
Kamal Ravikant

key takeaways

DO'S

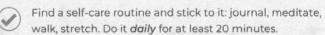 Find a self-care routine and stick to it: journal, meditate, walk, stretch. Do it *daily* for at least 20 minutes.

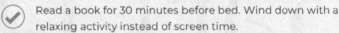 Read a book for 30 minutes before bed. Wind down with a relaxing activity instead of screen time.

Listen to calming music for 30 minutes. Soothing sounds can ease stress and promote relaxation.

DONT'S

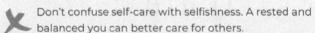 Don't confuse self-care with selfishness. A rested and balanced you can better care for others.

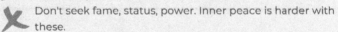 Don't seek fame, status, power. Inner peace is harder with these.

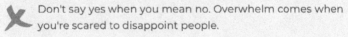 Don't say yes when you mean no. Overwhelm comes when you're scared to disappoint people.

part 14

nature

Inner peace is hard when you stay indoors most of
the time. Stay active. Stay outdoors. Explore.

Inner peace through nature

FREE TO WANDER

Albert Einstein, renowned for his genius in physics, found peace in nature's embrace.

One summer afternoon, overwhelmed by the complexities of his work, Einstein retreated to a quiet meadow near his home. As he lay beneath the swaying branches of a majestic oak tree, a sense of calm washed over him.

Gazing up at the vast expanse of sky above, Einstein marveled at the beauty and order of the universe. In that moment of stillness, he found clarity amidst the chaos of his thoughts.

It was here, in the tranquil embrace of nature, that Einstein's mind was free to wander and peaceful, untethered by the constraints of academia.

From that day forward, Einstein made a habit of escaping to nature whenever the weight of the world threatened to overwhelm him. For him, the secret to unlocking the mysteries of the universe lay not in textbooks or equations, but in the timeless wisdom of the natural world.

By discovering
nature,
you discover
yourself.
Maxime Lagacé

beyond nature

I took a walk in the woods and
came out taller than the trees.
Henry David Thoreau

And into the forest I go to lose
my mind and find my soul.
John Muir

Time spent amongst trees is
never time wasted. Katrina
Mayer

In every walk with nature
one receives far more
than he seeks. John Muir

learn from nature

GO SLOW

Adopt the pace of nature. Her secret is patience. Ralph Waldo Emerson

GO HOME

Going to the mountains is going home. John Muir

GO TO HEAVEN

Heaven is under our feet as well as over our heads. Henry David Thoreau

175

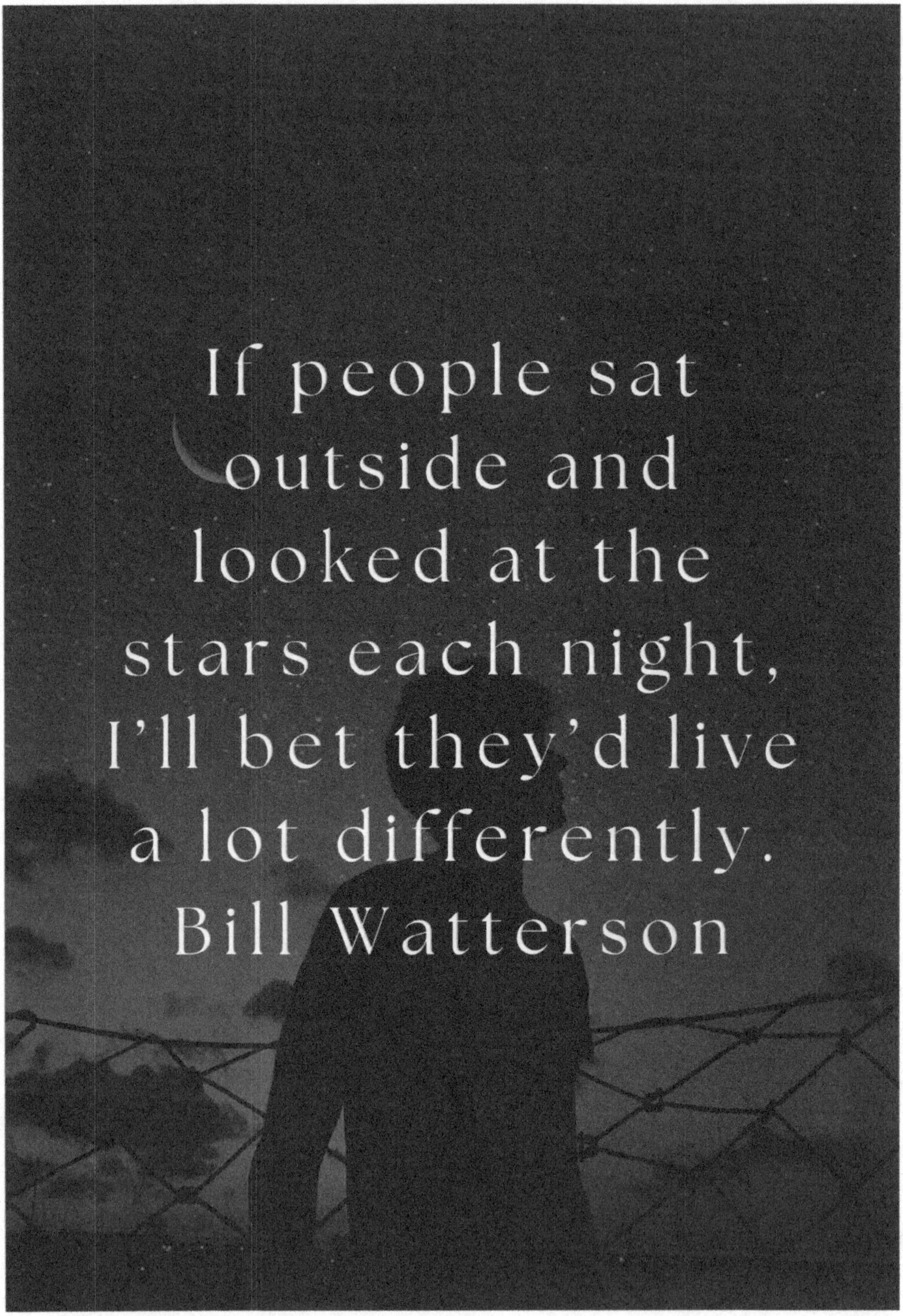

If people sat
outside and
looked at the
stars each night,
I'll bet they'd live
a lot differently.
Bill Watterson

the heart of the child

The sun illuminates only the eye of the man,
but shines into the eye and the heart of the child.

Ralph Waldo Emerson

infinitely healing

There is something infinitely healing
in the repeated refrains of nature –
the assurance that dawn comes after
night, and spring after winter.

Rachel Carson

observe

Look into nature, and then you will understand it better.

Albert Einstein

nature is simple

There I feel that nothing can befall me. Ralph Waldo Emerson

I felt my lungs inflate with the onrush of scenery – air, mountains, trees, people. I thought, "This is what it is to be happy". Sylvia Plath

Those who contemplate the beauty of the earth find reserves of strength that will endure as long as life lasts. Rachel Carson

THINK ABOUT THAT

Man's heart away from nature becomes hard. Standing Bear

I go to nature to be soothed and healed, and to have my senses put in order. John Burroughs

the power of nature

Nature abhors a vacuum, and if I can only walk with sufficient carelessness I am sure to be filled. Henry David Thoreau

If you will stay close to nature, to its simplicity, to the small things hardly noticeable, those things can unexpectedly become great and immeasurable. Rainer Maria Rilke

There's a whole world out there, right outside your window. You'd be a fool to miss it. Charlotte Eriksson

key takeaways

DO'S

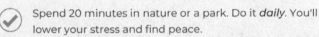 Spend 20 minutes in nature or a park. Do it *daily*. You'll lower your stress and find peace.

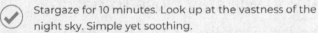 Stargaze for 10 minutes. Look up at the vastness of the night sky. Simple yet soothing.

 Adopt the pace of nature. Go s...l...o...wwww today.

DONT'S

 Don't stay indoors for too long. You are evolutionarily wired to move and explore outdoors.

 Don't bring your phone when walking outside. Disconnect to experience all the restorative benefits of nature.

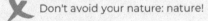 Don't avoid your nature: nature!

part 15

solitude

There will be moments of solitude in your life. Many
of them. Make sure you're comfortable with yourself.

Inner peace through solitude

INTO THE WILDERNESS

<u>John Muir</u>, the naturalist who championed America's National Parks, wasn't just an explorer. He craved solitude in nature. City life felt stifling, his mind cluttered with noise and obligations.

One day, at the young age of 29, he decided on a radical step. He packed a backpack and walked a thousand miles through the wilderness. Alone with the wind and the trees, a calmness washed over him.

Solitude wasn't about isolation, it was about reconnecting. He spent hours observing animals, sketching landscapes, and feeling a deep connection to the natural world. John returned with a renewed sense of purpose and a newfound peace.

In sum, he learned that inner peace wasn't found in crowded places, but in the quiet embrace of nature, a place where he could truly hear himself think.

Knowing yourself is the beginning of all wisdom. Aristotle

find answers

Solitude helps you find peace.
Peace helps you find
happiness. Maxime Lagacé

Be alone and be happy with
yourself. Leo Babauta

In solitude I find my answers.
Kristen Butler

When you discover that
all happiness is inside
you, the wanting and
needing are over, and life
gets very exciting. Byron
Katie

solitude is not loneliness

SIT QUIETLY
All of humanity's problems stem from man's inability to sit quietly in a room alone. Blaise Pascal

CLARIFY YOUR THOUGHTS
Solitude is the place of purification. Martin Buber

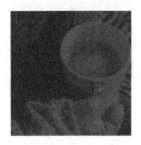

LEARN ABOUT YOURSELF
A little while alone in your room will prove more valuable than anything else that could ever be given you. Rumi

If I really want inner peace in my life, then I must not busy myself with what other people do and say.
Sri Chinmoy

it's your road

It's your road and yours alone.
Others may walk it with you,
but no one can walk it for you.

Rumi

your soul is free

Solitude is not the absence of
company, but the moment when our
soul is free to speak to us and help us
decide what to do with our life.

Paulo Coelho

sit, think

Never be afraid to sit awhile and think.

Lorraine Hansberry

192

a greater mind

Solitude is the great teacher, and to learn its lessons you must pay attention to it. Deepak Chopra

No one saves us but ourselves. No one can and no one may. We ourselves must walk the path. Buddha

The mind is sharper and keener in seclusion and uninterrupted solitude. Nikola Tesla

THINK ABOUT THAT

Solitude is a kind of freedom. Umberto Eco

In order to understand the world, one has to turn away from it on occasion. Albert Camus

More white spaces, more clarity, more inner peace. Maxime Lagacé

solitude simplifies

Solitude vivifies; isolation kills.
Joseph Roux

They who do not fear darkness
have learned to light their own
candle. Dodinsky

The more you enjoy solitude,
the simpler life becomes.
Maxime Lagacé

key takeaways

DO'S

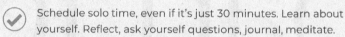 Schedule solo time, even if it's just 30 minutes. Learn about yourself. Reflect, ask yourself questions, journal, meditate.

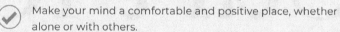 Make your mind a comfortable and positive place, whether alone or with others.

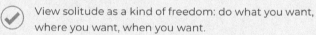 View solitude as a kind of freedom: do what you want, where you want, when you want.

DONT'S

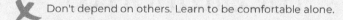 Don't depend on others. Learn to be comfortable alone.

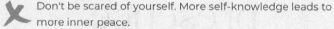 Don't be scared of yourself. More self-knowledge leads to more inner peace.

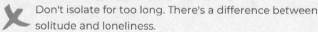 Don't isolate for too long. There's a difference between solitude and loneliness.

part 16

mindfulness &
meditation &
presence

Inner peace is only possible when you're mindful
and present, to yourself, to your friends,
to the world.

Inner peace through meditation

A GROUNDING RITUAL

The pre-game jitters. Every athlete knew them. Kobe Bryant, the Black Mamba himself, wasn't immune. His stomach churned, his mind racing through plays and scenarios. But Kobe had a secret weapon – meditation.

One morning, before a crucial game, the locker room buzzed with nervous energy. Kobe, though, was different. He slipped away, found a quiet corner, and closed his eyes. Breathe in, breathe out. He focused on his breath, letting go of worries, anxieties, even the plays themselves. Just him and the present moment.

Ten minutes later, Kobe emerged, a calmness radiating from him. His teammates, noticing the shift, exchanged curious glances. Kobe, with a clear mind and a laser focus, went on to dominate the game.

After the win, reporters swarmed him, but Kobe just smiled. "Meditation," he said simply. "It keeps me in the zone." From that day on, whispers of Kobe's "secret practice" spread. Maybe there was more to this meditation thing than anyone thought.

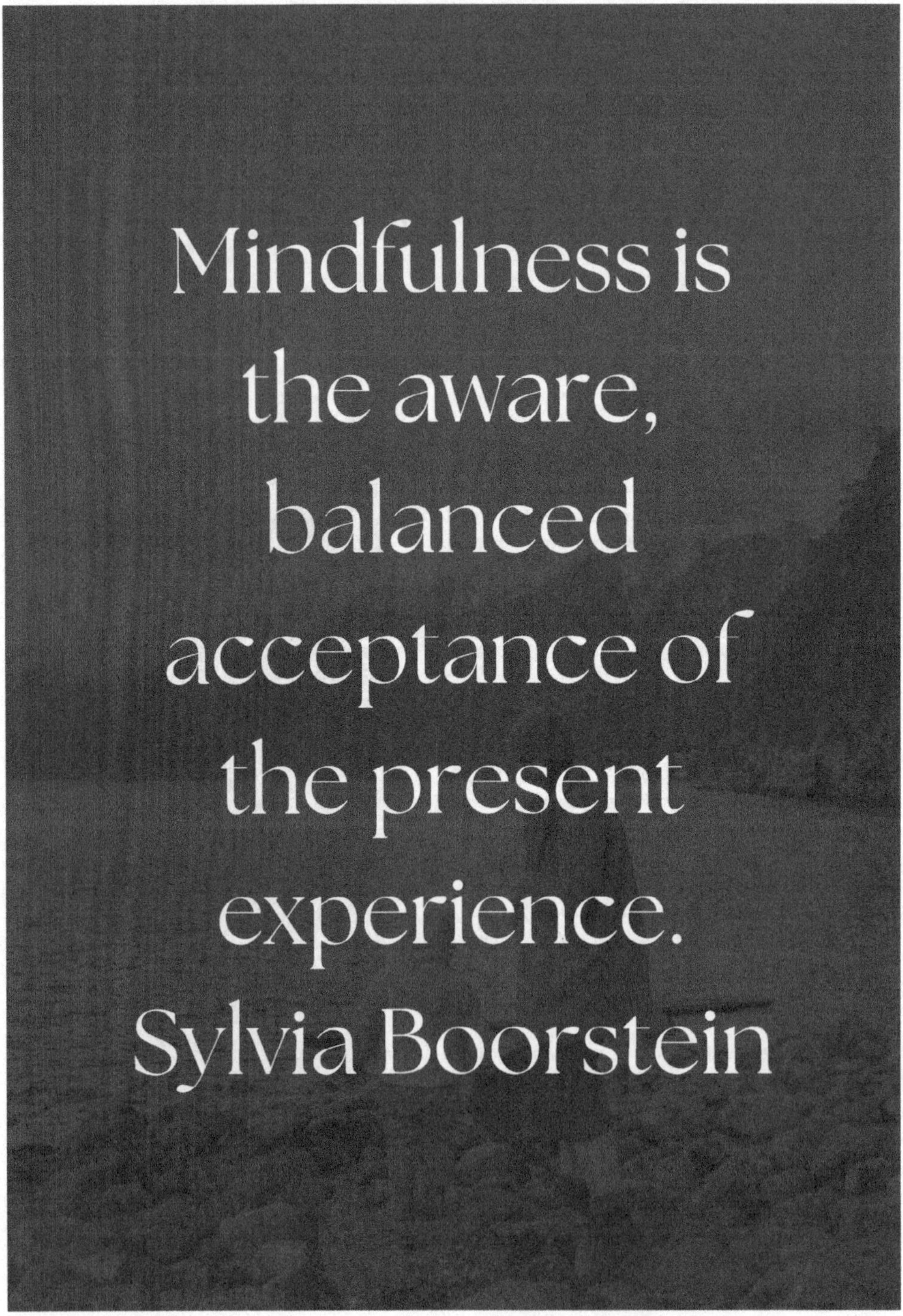

Mindfulness is
the aware,
balanced
acceptance of
the present
experience.
Sylvia Boorstein

be totally here

The quieter you become, the
more you can hear. Ram Dass

More patience, more presence,
less anxiety. Naval Ravikant

There is a great beauty in
observation, in seeing things
as they are. Jiddu Krishnamurti

Mindfulness is a way of
befriending ourselves and our
experience. Jon Kabat-Zinn

The more I meditate,
the easier life becomes.
Maxime Lagacé

be at ease

IT'S A GIFT
Give yourself a gift: the present moment. Marcus Aurelius

WHATEVER ARISES
Meditation is not about achieving anything. It's about letting go, being at ease with whatever arises. Andy Puddicombe

WORK WITH IT
Whatever the present moment contains, accept it as if you had chosen it. Always work with it, not against it. Eckhart Tolle

Wherever you are, be all there. Ram Dass

aware of what is

Don't hurry anything. Don't worry about the future.
Don't worry about what progress you're making.
Just be entirely content to be aware of what is.

Alan Watts

joy, peace, genius

The purpose of meditation is to
create the necessary inner ambience
for you to live in joy, peace, and in
turn unfold your genius.

Sadhguru

not candy, gold

In trading the pleasures of an ordinary life for a meditative life,
you're trading candy for gold.

Thanissaro Bhikkhu

205

play, now

A happy man is too satisfied with the present to dwell too much on the future. Albert Einstein

Anxiety, the illness of our time, comes primarily from our inability to dwell in the present moment. Thich Nhat Hanh

Sit just to enjoy your sitting; you don't need to attain any goal. Each moment of sitting meditation brings you back to life. Thich Nhat Hanh

THINK ABOUT THAT

A serious mind can never be in the present. Only a playful mind, only children, are in the present. So be more childlike... play more. Osho

Relax. Whatever it is, you're probably taking it too seriously. Ryan Holiday

be one with reality

In mindfulness one is not only
restful and happy, but alert
and awake. Meditation is not
evasion; it is a serene
encounter with reality. Thich
Nhat Hanh

When you understand yourself
you become calm. One way to
understand yourself is to
meditate. Maxime Lagacé

Whatever is fluid, soft, and
yielding will overcome
whatever is rigid and hard.
What is soft is strong. Lao Tzu

key takeaways

DO'S

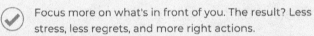 Focus more on what's in front of you. The result? Less stress, less regrets, and more right actions.

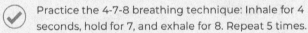 Practice the 4-7-8 breathing technique: Inhale for 4 seconds, hold for 7, and exhale for 8. Repeat 5 times.

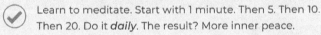 Learn to meditate. Start with 1 minute. Then 5. Then 10. Then 20. Do it *daily*. The result? More inner peace.

DONT'S

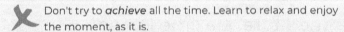 Don't try to *achieve* all the time. Learn to relax and enjoy the moment, as it is.

 Don't hurry. Stress only exists in your mind, not in nature.

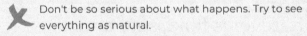 Don't be so serious about what happens. Try to see everything as natural.

part 17

self-understanding & self-knowledge

The more self-understanding and self-knowledge
you have, the calmer you become
in any given situation.

209

Inner peace through self-understanding

KEEP PAINTING, KEEP LEARNING

Actor <u>Jim Carrey</u>, the king of over-the-top comedy, wasn't always known for his zen demeanor. Early fame brought a whirlwind of success, but also a nagging emptiness. He chased the next laugh, the next project, but true happiness remained elusive.

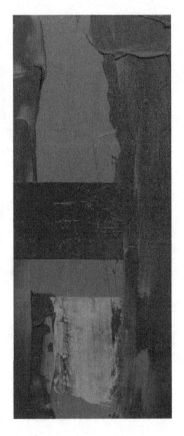

One day, a friend introduced him to painting. At first, it was messy and chaotic, mirroring Jim's inner state. But as he kept at it, something shifted. Focusing on the canvas, the brushstrokes became a form of meditation.

Through self-expression, Jim gained a deeper understanding of himself. He discovered a quieter side, a wellspring of creativity beyond the manic characters. Inner peace wasn't about hiding his goofy side, but about accepting all parts of himself. Jim learned that true happiness comes from knowing who you are, on and off the stage.

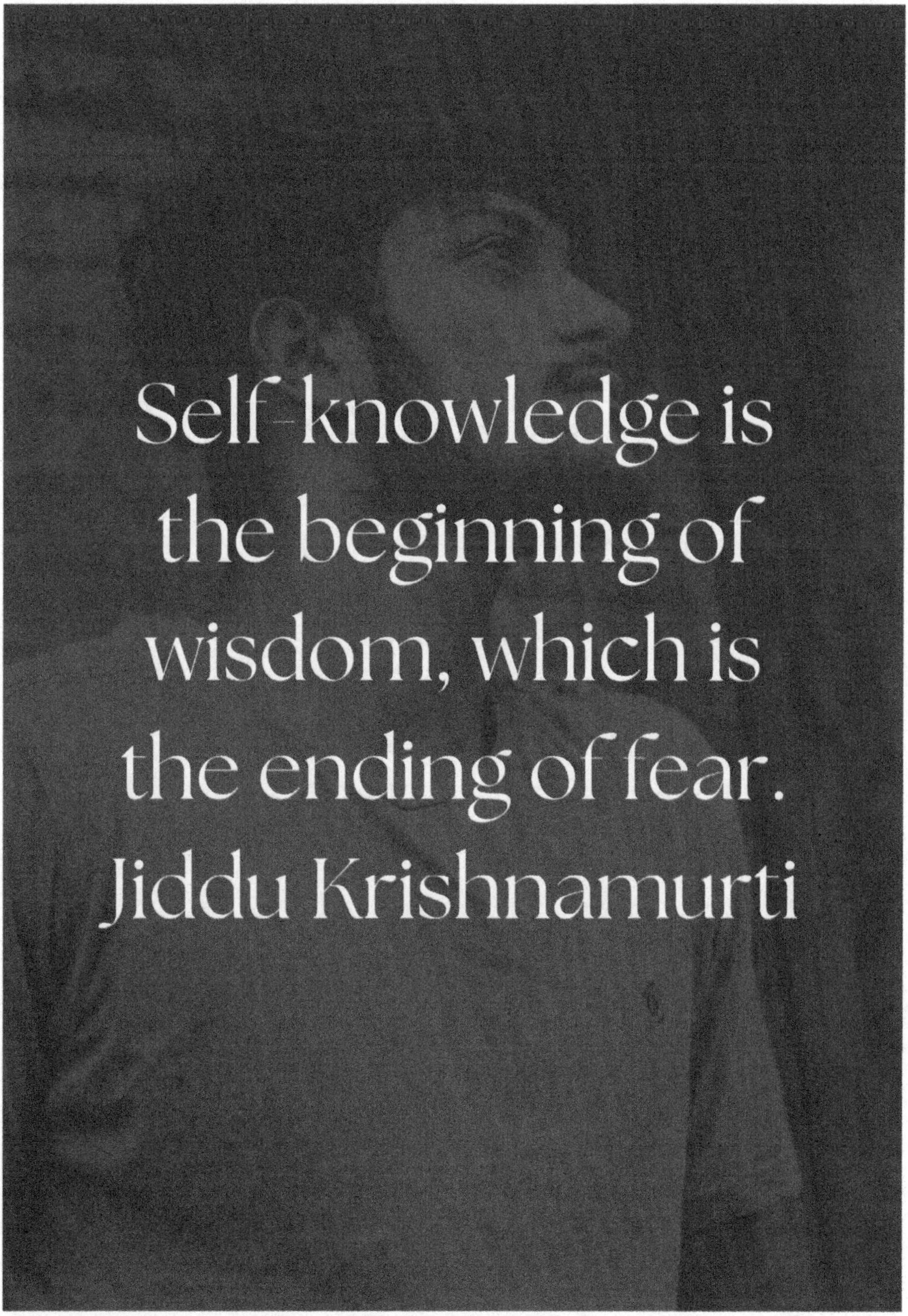

Self-knowledge is
the beginning of
wisdom, which is
the ending of fear.
Jiddu Krishnamurti

know yourself

Self-understanding leads to inner peace. Maxime Lagacé

Understanding is the first step to acceptance, and only with acceptance can there be recovery. J. K. Rowling

The noblest pleasure is the joy of understanding. Leonardo da Vinci

The moment you know
yourself you have known
the most precious thing
in existence. Osho

understand your...

YOUR SOUL
A person will understand his place in the world only when he understands his soul. Chinese wisdom

YOUR ROOTS
Maybe you are searching among the branches, for what only appears in the roots. Rumi

YOUR HISTORY
A people without the knowledge of their past history, origin and culture is like a tree without roots. Marcus Garvey

214

If you could only know who you are, all your troubles would seem utterly unnecessary and trivial. Leo Tolstoy

the inner law

The purpose of your life is not to do as the majority does,
but to live according to the inner law
which you understand in yourself.

Marcus Aurelius

it's every moment

Self-understanding is an enormous task.
It is not to be done casually, later on,
tomorrow, but rather every day,
every moment, all the time.

Jiddu Krishnamurti

calmness

Calmness follows order which follows understanding.

Maxime Lagacé

it's within yourself

Be faithful to that which exists within yourself. André Gide

To go wrong in one's own way is better than to go right in someone else's. Fyodor Dostoevsky

When I discover who I am, I'll be free. Ralph Ellison

THINK ABOUT THAT

Happiness is self-connectedness. Aristotle

To know yourself you need not go to any book, to any priest, to any psychologist. The whole treasure is within yourself. Jiddu Krishnamurti

it's a journey

One who knows others is intelligent. One who knows himself is enlightened. Lao Tzu

Understanding comes through awareness. Alan Watts

When will you begin that long journey into yourself? Rumi

key takeaways

DO'S

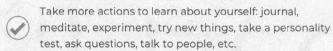 Take more actions to learn about yourself: journal, meditate, experiment, try new things, take a personality test, ask questions, talk to people, etc.

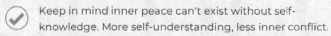 Keep in mind inner peace can't exist without self-knowledge. More self-understanding, less inner conflict.

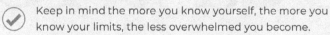 Keep in mind the more you know yourself, the more you know your limits, the less overwhelmed you become.

DONT'S

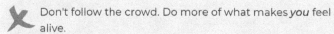 Don't follow the crowd. Do more of what makes *you* feel alive.

Don't escape yourself. Listen to your little voice. This leads to less fear and more confidence.

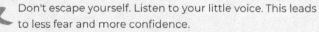 Don't depend on anyone. Learn about self-reliance (See Ralph Waldo Emerson)

part 18

healing

You may have been hurt before. To know inner peace, you must heal from your past.

Inner peace through healing

FORGIVE, THEN MOVE ON

Consider the journey of <u>Nelson Mandela</u>, the former president of South Africa. Mandela spent 27 years in prison, enduring harsh conditions and isolation. Yet, during his incarceration, he discovered a profound sense of inner peace and healing.

Despite facing immense injustice and suffering, Mandela chose to forgive his oppressors and embrace reconciliation rather than seek revenge. Through his unwavering commitment to peace and forgiveness, Mandela not only healed himself but also helped heal a nation torn apart by racial division.

Mandela's story teaches you that inner peace and healing are possible even in the most challenging circumstances. By choosing forgiveness and reconciliation over bitterness and resentment, you can find true healing and happiness in your life, no matter what obstacles you face.

Before healing
others, heal yourself.
Gambian saying

steps to healing

1. If we are to nurture and heal, we must admit that the wounds exist. Iyanla Vanzant

2. Stop looking for happiness in the same place you lost it. Paulo Coelho

3. If you understand the problem, you can solve the problem. Sahil Lavingia

Unlearn all that you have
learned up to now. Forget
your past, disconnect
yourself, don't look back.
Look in the moment, in the
present, and be in a totally
relaxed state, available.
Osho

healing is...

AFFIRMING YOUR LIMITS

Healing starts when you're clear about your limits. It starts when you say no. It starts when you have space to be. Then you stop feeling overwhelmed.

ACCEPTING THE PAIN

You must let the pain visit. You must allow it teach you. You must not allow it to overstay.

MOVING FORWARD

Healing doesn't mean the damage never existed. It means the damage *no longer* controls your life.

It's okay to not be okay. It's okay to take a pause in life.

the greatest gift

The worst loss you've ever experienced
is the greatest gift you can have.

Byron Katie

start building the new

You will never find peace standing
in the ruins of what you used to be.
You can only move on if you start
building something new.

Brianna Wiest

the door will open

The moment you accept what troubles you've been given,
the door will open.

Rumi

find healing

As confusion disappears, so does suffering. Ringu Tulku

Simplicity begins when you stop believing everything you think. Courtney Carver

Nature heals. Mediation heals. Walking heals. A friend heals. Exercise heals. Journaling heals. Find what heals you. Maxime Lagacé

THINK ABOUT THAT

The key to dealing with pain is not minding that it hurts. Ed Latimore

These pains you feel are messengers. Listen to them. Rumi

Change the person in the mirror, and your world will change. Rhonda Byrne

keys to healing

Be like a tree and let the dead
leaves drop. Rumi

Don't try to fill your void with
noise. Fill it with silence.
Maxime Lagacé

We are healed of a suffering
only by experiencing it to the
full. Marcel Proust

key takeaways

DO'S

 Practice saying no to commitments that drain your energy. Prioritize activities that nourish your well-being.

 Remember inner peace is when you accept the past and the present, as they are.

 Talk to a friend, a therapist, or a support group. Clarify the situation. Move forward.

DONT'S

 Don't escape your problem. Face it, calmly. Ask for help if you need.

 Don't be scared to create a new you. You have no obligation to be who you were 5 minutes ago.

 Don't rush the process. Healing takes time and is not linear. Be patient with yourself.

part 19

love &
compassion

Once you know yourself, and once you have
healed, the next step is to show love.

Inner peace through love

A HUG, A GENTLE WORD

<u>Mister Rogers</u>, the beloved host of Mister Rogers' Neighborhood, wasn't just about puppets and catchy songs. He believed in the inherent goodness of everyone, even grumpy neighbors and shy children.

Filming could be stressful, but Fred Rogers, the man behind the persona, focused on compassion. He'd take time after shows to talk to upset kids, offering a hug and a gentle word.

Inner peace, for him, wasn't about being perfect. It came from seeing the best in people, offering kindness even on difficult days.

Mister Rogers' legacy reminds us that true happiness lies in showing compassion, making the world a little brighter, one person at a time.

236

Where there is love
there is life.
Mahatma Gandhi

a loving heart

In the end we discover that to love and let go can be the same thing. Jack Kornfield

A loving heart is the truest wisdom. Charles Dickens

One word frees us of all the weight and pain of life: that word is love. Sophocles

The more I think it over,
the more I feel that there
is nothing more truly
artistic than to love
people. Vincent van Gogh

love is...

THE BEST PATH
To love is risky. Not to love is foolish. Maxime Lagacé

THE BEST GIFT
Even better than being loved is being in love. Naval Ravikant

THE BEST ADVENTURE
We love because it's the only true adventure. Nikki Giovanni

Better to have loved and lost, than to have never loved at all. Augustine of Hippo

everything you want

Knowing, understanding, and loving yourself
is your first step to everything you want in life.

Maxime Lagacé

joy, bliss

The best thing you can do for the
world is to be a joyful
and blissful human being.

Sadhguru

listen

The first duty of love is to listen.

Paul Tillich

244

you love, you win

Every thing that you love, you will eventually lose, but in the end, love will return in a different form. Franz Kafka

Love is never lost. If not reciprocated, it will flow back and soften and purify the heart. Washington Irving

You never lose by loving. You always lose by holding back. Barbara De Angelis

THINK ABOUT THAT

There is no remedy for love but to love more. Henry David Thoreau

We must be our own before we can be another's. Ralph Waldo Emerson

love, dance, sing

Love is the greatest refreshment in life. Pablo Picasso

You've gotta dance like there's nobody watching, love like you'll never be hurt, sing like there's nobody listening, and live like it's heaven on earth. William W. Purkey

Never bend your head. Always hold it high. Look the world straight in the face. Helen Keller

key takeaways

DO'S

 Treat other people, and yourself, with dignity, respect, and love.

 Practice active listening. Put away distractions and truly focus on what the other person is saying.

 Hold the door open for someone. Random acts of kindness can make a big difference.

DONT'S

 Don't think you'll find peace by avoiding life.

 Don't hold grudges. Letting go of resentment allows you to live free.

 Don't mind if people watch. Be free. Dance, sing, love.

part 20

focus &
discipline &
self-control

Inner peace is knowing what must be done,
and doing it. It's also being able to focus
and having self-control.

Inner peace through discipline

A RITUAL

Imagine staring at a blank canvas every day. That was <u>Georgia O'Keeffe</u>, the famous painter known for her bold florals. But anxiety wasn't her friend. Self-doubt swirled sometimes.

Instead of panicking, Georgia had a ritual. Each morning, she'd wake up before dawn, the quiet a blank canvas itself. She'd meditate, focusing on her breath, calming the noise in her head. Then, she'd paint. Disciplined strokes, one by one.

The anxiety didn't vanish, but it didn't control her. With focus and a calm mind, Georgia transformed her struggles into vibrant masterpieces.

For her, inner peace wasn't the absence of worry, it was the quiet strength to work through it.

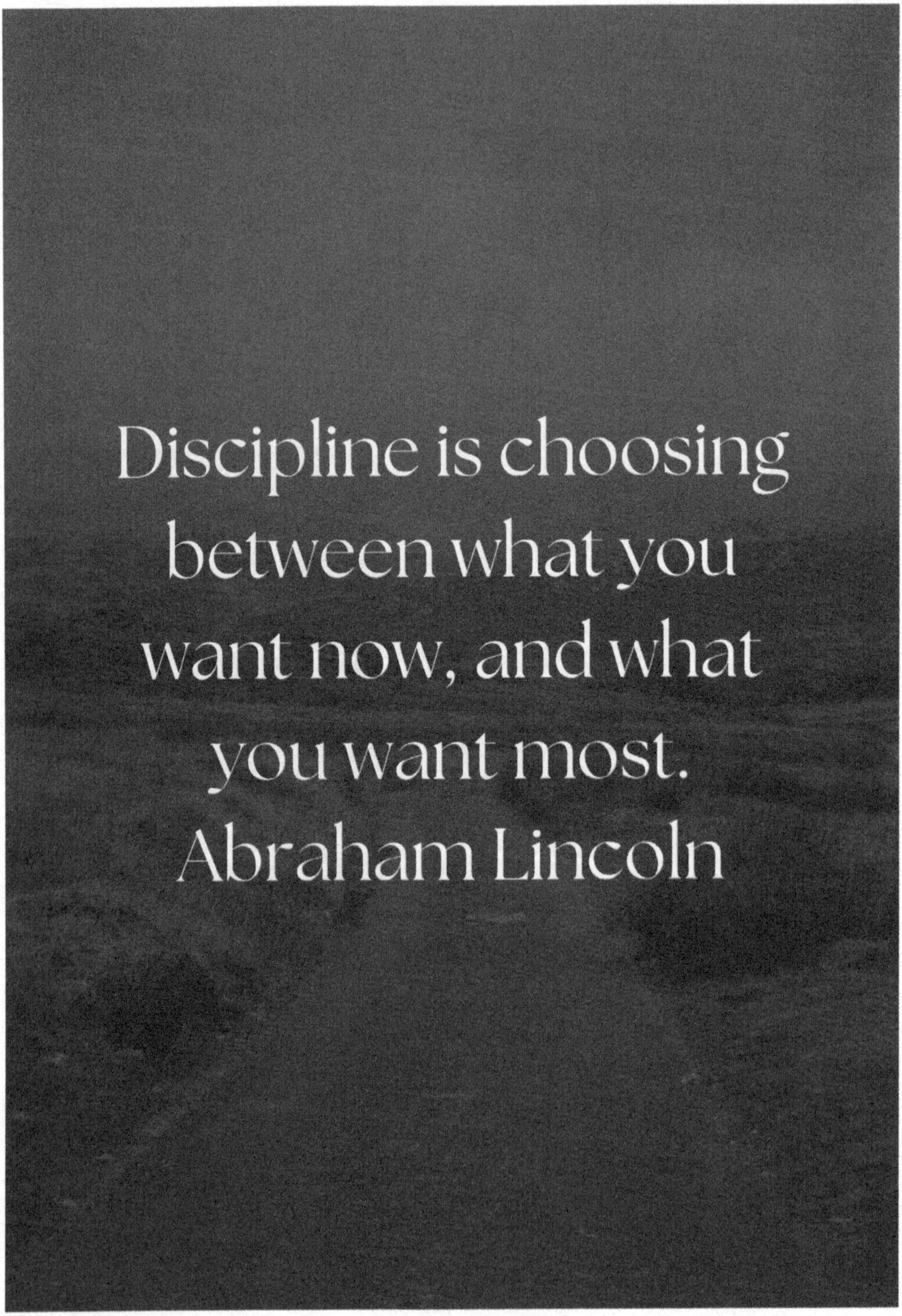

Discipline is choosing
between what you
want now, and what
you want most.
Abraham Lincoln

discipline is...

Discipline is remembering what you want. David Campbell

Discipline means creating an order within you. Osho

Discipline is short-term pains for long-term gains. Maxime Lagacé

As far as your self-control
goes, as far goes your
freedom. Marie Ebner

calm your mind

MAKE IT YOUR SERVANT
Rule your mind, which, if it is not your servant, is your master.
Horace

MAKE IT FOCUSED
Remember: our business is with things that really matter. Marcus Aurelius

MAKE IT CALM
If you can win over your mind, you can win over the whole world.
Sri Sri Ravi Shankar

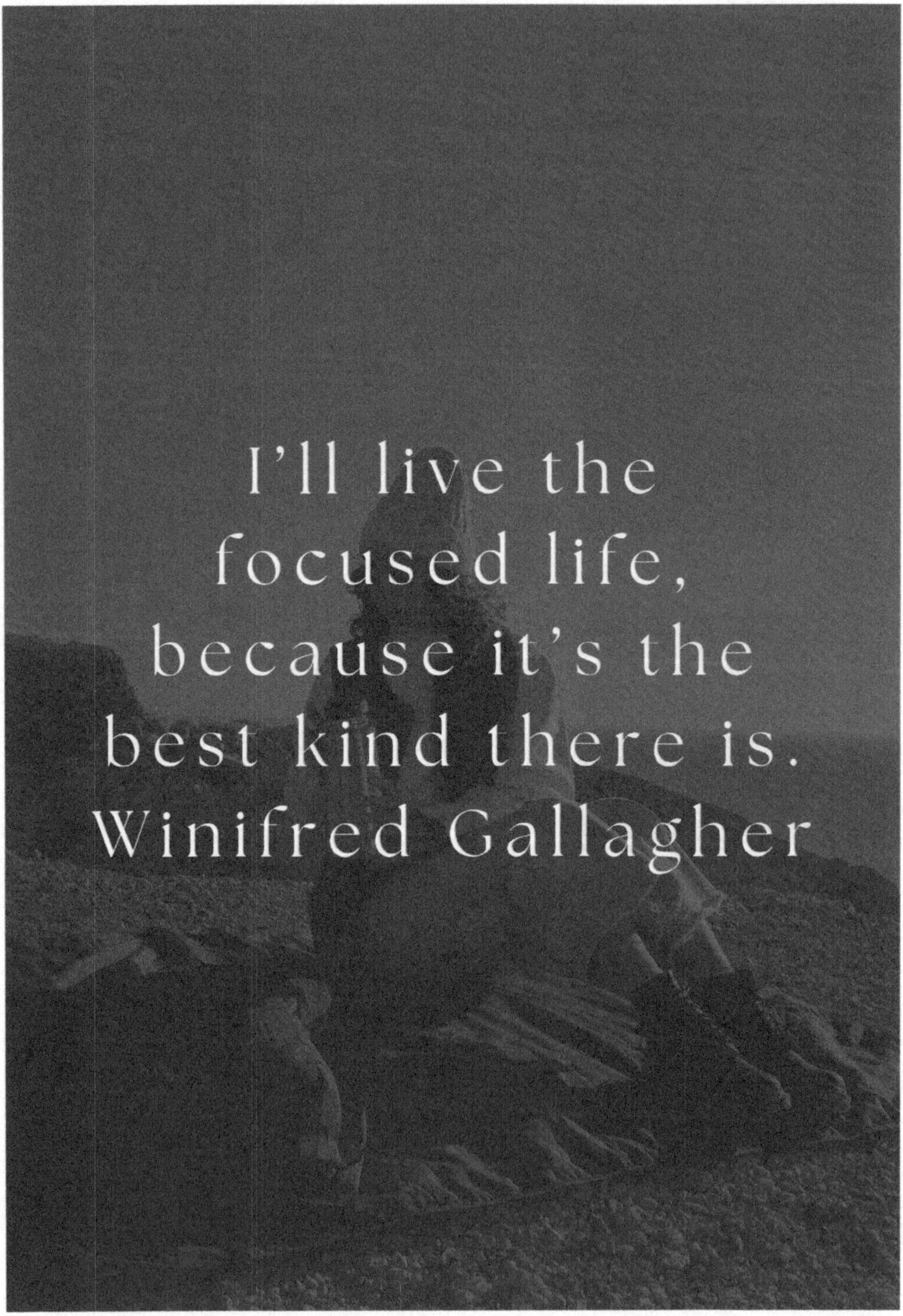

I'll live the
focused life,
because it's the
best kind there is.
Winifred Gallagher

do the hard thing

The senses have been conditioned by attraction
to the pleasant and aversion to the unpleasant.
Do not be ruled by them.

Bhagavad Gita

it hurts, but it's fine

Discipline is conditioning your brain to stay indifferent if it's hard, or if it hurts. If it needs to get done, it gets done.

Mark Manson

focus your mind

Every hour focus your mind attentively...on the performance of
the task in hand, with dignity, human sympathy, benevolence
and freedom, and leave aside all other thoughts.

Marcus Aurelius

do what must be done

Self-reverence, self-knowledge, self-control, These three alone lead life to sovereign power. Alfred Tennyson

He who cannot obey himself will be commanded. That is the nature of living creatures. Friedrich Nietzsche

The poorest education that teaches self-control is better than the best that neglects it. Dorothy Nevill

control yourself

In the twenty-first century,
survival of the fittest means
survival of the focused.
Giovanni Dienstmann

The intelligent desire self-
control; children want candy.
Rumi

Not being able to govern
events, I govern myself. Michel
de Montaigne

key takeaways

 Do what you know should be done. Do it again tomorrow.

 Focus on your most important task for 60 minutes, then take a 5-minute break. Then repeat. Be in "monk mode."

 Exercise for 30 minutes most days of the week. Physical activity enhances your cognitive function and willpower.

DONT'S

 Don't skip two days in a row. Aim for consistency.

 Don't think a peaceful life is about comfort. It's more about acceptance, focus, and responsibility.

 Don't say "yes" easily (to requests, distractions, etc.). Inner peace requires saying no to the unimportant.

part 21

materialism

Most of us seek happiness and contentment
through consumption and materialism.
But the wisest know it can't be achieved this way.

Inner peace with less stuff

EXPERIENCES, NOT THINGS

Leonardo DiCaprio, the famous actor, could buy anything money can buy: fancy cars, designer clothes, the whole package. But after years of chasing possessions, Leo felt a deep emptiness.

One day, filming on a remote island, a local villager showed him a different way. The villager had next to nothing, yet exuded a genuine peace Leo envied. It sparked a change.

Leo started focusing on experiences, not things. He traveled to see the world's beauty and volunteered for environmental causes. Slowly, that empty feeling faded.

He realized inner peace wasn't found in material things, but in connecting with something bigger than himself.

Materialism and all its miseries can never be conquered by materialism.
Swami Vivekananda

value the right things

No one is impressed with your possessions as much as you are. Morgan Housel

The things you own end up owning you. Chuck Palahniuk

The more we value things, the less we value ourselves. Bruce Lee

The fundamental
delusion - there is
something out there that
will make me happy and
fulfilled forever. Naval
Ravikant

materialism is...

AN IDENTITY CRISIS
Materialism is an identity crisis.
Bryant H. McGill

KFC FOR YOUR SOUL
Materialism is KFC for the soul.
Johann Hari

ALWAYS WANTING MORE
Materialism: believing stuff will
make you happy. Maxime Lagacé

266

One day you will
realize that
material things
mean nothing.
All that matters is
the well-being of
the people in your
life.

liberate yourself

A person can understand his real destination in life
only after he manages to liberate himself
from the sensual, material world.

Leo Tolstoy

let go of stuff

It is the preoccupation with
possessions, more than anything else,
that prevents us from living freely
and nobly.

Bertrand Russell

true power

Buying things gives us a false sense of control.
True power is realizing you don't need much.

Maxime Lagacé

270

simple life, happy life

Happiness does not come from consumption of things. Thich Nhat Hanh

Those who lose themselves in their desire for possession lose their innate nature. Zhuangzi

Almost nothing material is needed for a happy life, for he who has understood existence. Marcus Aurelius

THINK ABOUT THAT

If you can't be happy with a coffee, you won't be happy with a yacht. Naval Ravikant

Materialism: A tendency to consider material possessions and physical comfort as more important than spiritual values.

Activities connect us to others; objects often separate us. Jonathan Haidt

less stuff, less stress

What if the answer isn't to do more? What if the answer is to want less? Mark Manson

Less stuff, less clutter, less stress. Maxime Lagacé

Happiness is a quality of the soul...not a function of one's material circumstances. Aristotle

key takeaways

DO'S

 Practice the "one in, one out" rule: For each new item you bring into your home, donate or discard one item.

Buy experiences instead of stuff. Less stuff equals more freedom.

Remember you'll never have enough. You'll never say "That's it. I'm happy. I'm done."

DONT'S

 Don't think happiness is buying stuff. Happiness is a direction. Happiness is a skill you develop.

 Don't forget the more stuff you have, the more overwhelmed you'll feel.

 Don't think "power" is having more. Power is being satisfied with less.

part 22

technology &
social media &
smartphones

To keep your inner peace and avoid being
overwhelmed, make sure you use your tools, and
that your tools don't use you.

Inner peace by doing a digital detox

LESS FOMO (FEAR OF MISSING OUT)

DJ Khaled, famous music producer, battled anxiety for years. He'd constantly check his phone, worried about missing a beat or a message. But it took a toll on his well-being.

One day, he decided on a digital detox. Less phone usage, less scrolling, no late-night email spirals, etc. Instead, he focused on mindfulness exercises and spending quality time with his family.

The change was dramatic. Khaled reported feeling calmer, more present in the moment. He even started incorporating mindfulness techniques into his music, creating a more Zen vibe for his fans.

The experience showed him that inner peace wasn't about ignoring the digital world, but about creating healthy boundaries with it.

Technology was
supposed to free us.
It seems to have
mainly bound us.

technology is great, but...

The human brain isn't designed to process all of the world's emergencies in realtime. Naval Ravikant

In solving problems, technology creates new problems, and we seem to have to keep running faster and faster to stay where we are. Alan Watts

The only way to make peace with technology is to make peace with ourselves. Tristan Harris

The miracles of technology cause us to live in a hectic, clockwork world that does violence to human biology. Alan Watts

moderation

YOU'LL ALWAYS NEED MORE
Entertainment becomes boring if not constrained. Angela Jiang

A BUFFET
The Internet is a buffet. Eat but do not be gluttonous. You'll get sick.

THE MODERN DEVIL
The modern devil is cheap dopamine. Naval Ravikant

Do not waste your days living for other people's validation on social media.
Gal Shapira

the Internet is great, but...

The Internet is as useful
as your self-control.

Shane Parrish

turn your phone off

Today is a great day to turn your phone off, go outside, take a walk, read a good book, and remember that the world is not social media.

Steve Magness

take control

The more time teens spend looking at screens, the more likely
they are to report symptoms of depression. Jean M. Twenge

Jean M. Twenge

don't "smoke" too much

The smartphone is the modern-day hypodermic needle, delivering digital dopamine 24/7 for a wired generation. Anna Lembke

Modern technology is made to keep you addicted. Addiction is the end game. Profit is what they seek. Jose Rosado

Our minds have been hijacked by technology. Tristan Harris

Our brains are not evolved for this world of plenty. Anna Lembke

THINK ABOUT THAT

Scrolling is the new smoking.
Sahil Lavingia

By bringing the world together, social media is tearing it apart.
Naval Ravikant

Because you live in an information tsunami does not mean you have to surf it. Brian Norgard

use your tools, don't let them use you

Practice social media distancing. Sahil Lavingia

Get off your phones, computers, and shut the TV off. Don't let this fast-paced world dull your sharpest weapon, that weapon being your mind. David Goggins

Disconnect from the world, connect with yourself. Dan Koe

key takeaways

DO'S

 Put your phone on airplane mode for the first 4 hours of the day.

 Establish a bedtime routine that includes turning off screens at least 60 minutes before sleep.

 Remember your brain needs free time, rest time, and play time to function properly. No break, no peace.

DONT'S

 Don't have more than 60 minutes of screen time per day. And spend at least 60 minutes outside. You were born to explore, not stare at a screen.

 Don't let your phone's notifications rule your life. Keep only the most vital ones.

 Don't forget the connection with the persons beside you is more important with the ones on your screen.

part 23

addictions &
bad habits

Having many addictions and bad habits leads to
ruin. Make sure you stay on the bright side.

Inner peace by slowing down

THERE'S NO RUSH

Charles Dickens, the famous writer, had an addiction. He was a workaholic. He'd pump out chapters late into the night, fueled by endless cups of coffee.

Stress took its toll. He got sick, anxious. Finally, his doctor gave him a simple advice: "If you don't slow down, you'll write yourself into an early grave."

Dickens listened. He cut back on coffee, started taking long walks. He even joined an amateur acting troupe, just for fun.

Slowly, the frantic energy calmed. He still wrote, but with a newfound peace. His characters, once a bit harried, gained a depth that resonated with readers even more.

Dickens learned that inner peace wasn't the enemy of creativity, it was the fuel.

Addiction is a progressive narrowing of the things that bring you pleasure.
Andrew Huberman

addiction is...

Addiction is an increasing desire for an act that gives less and less satisfaction. Aldous Huxley

In the same way as the storm troubles and muddies the waters, so too passions trouble our souls and interfere with our understanding of this life. Leo Tolstoy

With prolonged and repeated exposure to pleasurable stimuli, our capacity to tolerate pain decreases, and our threshold for experiencing pleasure increases. Anna Lembke

290

The relentless pursuit of
pleasure and avoidance
of pain, leads to pain.
Anna Lembke

it's endless

THE PURSUIT

In an age of abundance, the pursuit of pleasure for its own sake leads to addiction. Naval Ravikant

THE ENTERTAINMENT

We've lost the ability to tolerate even minor forms of discomfort. We're constantly seeking to distract ourselves from the present moment, to be entertained. Anna Lembke

THE PLEASURE

The majority of men are discontented with their life, and seek the pleasures of the flesh. But the flesh can never be satisfied, and men... seek oblivion in smoking or drunkenness. Leo Tolstoy

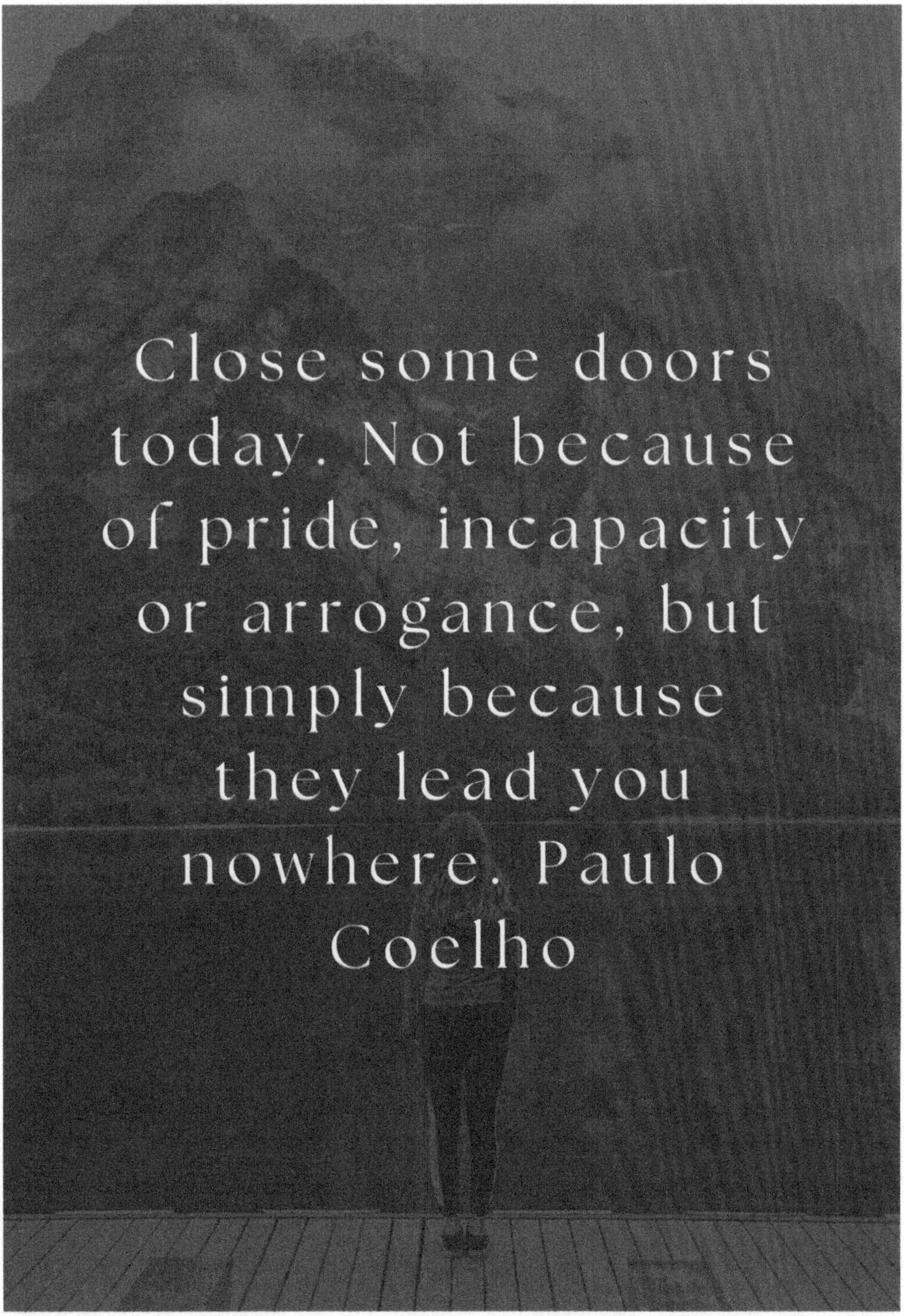

Close some doors
today. Not because
of pride, incapacity
or arrogance, but
simply because
they lead you
nowhere. Paulo
Coelho

digital addiction

Digital addiction is going to be
one of the great mental health crises of our time.

Sam Altman

"I've arrived!"

You will never, never be able to sit
back with full contentment and say,
"Now, I've arrived!".

Alan Watts

don't search outside

The roots of addiction can be seen in our search for happiness
in something outside of our self,
be it drugs, relationships, material possessions.

Lee L Jampolsky

296

keep yourself in check

We have so many drugs now, electronic and chemical, that most of us are junkies most of the time. Naval Ravikant

Abundance is harder for us to handle than scarcity. Nassim Nicholas Taleb

We must keep ourselves in check or risk ruin. Or imbalance. Or dysfunction. Or dependency. Ryan Holiday

THINK ABOUT THAT

Comfort is the worst addiction. Marcus Aurelius

The mind craves pleasure, and in doing so creates pain. James Pierce

The superior man thinks always of virtue; the common man thinks of comfort. Confucius

unplug

If you can't control your mind, everything and everyone else will. Joe Dispenza

It takes discipline not to let social media steal your time. Alexis Ohanian

Sorry to interrupt your scrolling, but are you ok? Unknown

Almost everything will work again if you unplug it for a few minutes, including you. Anne Lamott

key takeaways

DO'S

 Be realistic: admit you may have an addiction problem first.

 Be smart: ask for help if you need to. A problem shared is a problem halved.

 Learn to be comfortable with discomfort and boredom. Self-reliance and self-knowledge lead to calm and order.

DONT'S

 Don't be a slave. Learn to break bad habits. A simple trick is to make the habit harder to do. (See Atomic Habits)

 Don't say you feel tired and overwhelmed if you spend more than 60 minutes on your screens daily.

 Don't escape. Let yourself feel pain. Let go of your need to feel good all the time. It's human to feel bad.

part 24

distractions

Learn to find inner peace despite the distractions of the modern world.

300

Inner peace by focusing

WHEN YOU WORK, WORK. WHEN YOU PLAY, PLAY.

Zen master Shunryu Suzuki chopped vegetables for dinner. Each slice, each snip, was deliberate. His movements flowed with quiet focus.

A student interrupted, "Master, isn't meditation more important than chores?" Shunryu smiled. "When I cut vegetables," he said, "I cut vegetables. When I sweep the floor, I sweep the floor."

The student frowned. "But what about distracting thoughts?" Shunryu paused. "Thoughts are like passing clouds," he said gently. "I watch them come and go. But my attention stays here, on the task at hand."

The student watched, mesmerized, as Shunryu returned to chopping.

Inner peace, he realized, wasn't about silencing distractions, but choosing where to place your attention.

Too much sugar leads to a heavy body, and too many distractions lead to a heavy mind.
Naval Ravikant

choose wisely

There are always distractions, if
you allow them. Tony La Russa

Too many people believe that
everything must be
pleasurable in life, which
makes them constantly search
for distractions. Robert Greene

The modern world is a gift. It
gives us tools and choices, but
we need the self-discipline and
wisdom to choose wisely.
Naval Ravikant

You will never reach your
destination if you stop
and throw stones at
every dog that barks.
Winston Churchill

noise vs signal

DON'T GET DISTRACTED
90 percent of success is not
getting distracted. Shane Parrish

IGNORE THE NOISE
99.99% of everything is noise.
Michael Saylor

FOCUS
Focus is the art of knowing what
to ignore. James Clear

You get your life back the moment you learn to say no to almost everything. Greg McKeown

stay intelligent

Intelligence consists in ignoring things
that are irrelevant.

Nassim Nicholas Taleb

step out

Stepping out of the busyness is
perhaps the most beautiful offering
we can make to our spirit.

Tara Brach

cut the toxic

Cut the unnecessary distractions out of your life — delete apps,
unfriend and unfollow toxic people, stop committing to
activities you don't care about. Life is too short.

Mark Manson

guard your mind

Society wants your time, money, and attention. Guard them. Maxime Lagacé

The human brain evolved to prioritize immediate rewards over delayed rewards. James Clear

Dopamine and constant stimulation can impair your ability to think long-term. Thibaut Meurisse

laser-like focus

Most information is time-consuming, negative, irrelevant to your goals, and outside of your influence. Tim Ferriss

You get your life back the moment you learn to say no to almost everything. Greg McKeown

The successful warrior is the average man, with laser-like focus. Bruce Lee

The successful warrior is the average man, with laser-like focus. Bruce Lee

key takeaways

DO'S

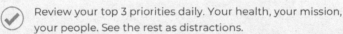 Review your top 3 priorities daily. Your health, your mission, your people. See the rest as distractions.

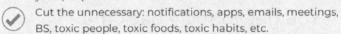 Cut the unnecessary: notifications, apps, emails, meetings, BS, toxic people, toxic foods, toxic habits, etc.

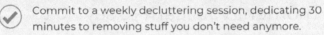 Commit to a weekly decluttering session, dedicating 30 minutes to removing stuff you don't need anymore.

DONT'S

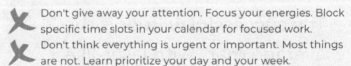 Don't give away your attention. Focus your energies. Block specific time slots in your calendar for focused work.

Don't think everything is urgent or important. Most things are not. Learn prioritize your day and your week.

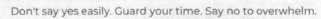 Don't say yes easily. Guard your time. Say no to overwhelm.

part 25

boredom

Boredom is fine.
In fact, the less affected you are by it,
the more peaceful you are.

Inner peace through boredom

PAY ATTENTION

Rain lashed against the cabin windows. Henry David Thoreau was stuck inside for days. No internet, no TV, just him and the storm.

Boredom gnawed at him. He paced, stared at the walls. Then, something shifted. He sat by the window, watching the rain.

The rhythm of the drops soothed him. He noticed the dance of leaves in the wind. He started writing, not about grand ideas, but the beauty of a single raindrop tracing a path down the glass.

The boredom became a blank canvas. It forced him to find peace in the simple, the overlooked. He discovered that sometimes, inner peace hides in the quiet moments, waiting to be noticed.

Boredom is the feeling that everything is a waste of time; serenity, that nothing is.
Thomas Szasz

boredom is...

Boredom: the desire for desires. Leo Tolstoy

Boredom is a defense mechanism to avoid having to sit alone with our unaddressed thoughts. Naval Ravikant

Boredom is the inevitable consequence of a life devoted to pleasure. Kapil Gupta

Boredom comes from
thinking this moment
isn't enough. James
Pierce

embrace boredom

ACCEPT THE MOMENT
He is really wise who is nettled at nothing. François de La Rochefoucauld

BE CURIOUS
I don't know anything, but I do know that everything is interesting if you go into it deeply enough. Richard Feynman

BE PEACEFUL
Happiness is loving the boring days. Thibaut

There is no
observable
difference between
peace and
boredom – only
your mindset.
Angela Jiang

calm and modest

A calm and modest life brings more happiness than
the pursuit of success combined
with constant restlessness.

Albert Einstein

stay independent

Decrease dopamine dependency.
Bring back boredom.

Anthony Pompliano

pay attention

When you pay attention to boredom
it gets unbelievably interesting.

Jon Kabat-Zinn

322

boredom is useful

Being bored is more useful than being busy. Maxime Lagacé

Boredom leads to one of these two things: more boredom or more creativity. Matthew Kobach

The key to unlocking productive deep work is to make peace with boredom. Cal Newport

THINK ABOUT THAT

Smartphones removed boredom at the cost of peace of mind.

The more you run from boredom, the more it follows you. James Pierce

the best thinking

A generation that cannot endure boredom will be a generation of little men... of men in whom every vital impulse slowly withers, as though they were cut flowers in a vase. Bertrand Russell

This great misfortune – to be incapable of solitude. Jean de La Bruyère

Escaping boredom leads to stress. Embracing boredom leads to peace. Maxime Lagacé

The best thinking has been done in solitude. Thomas A. Edison

key takeaways

DO'S

 Learn to be fine with boredom. Ideas come when you're relaxed.

 Be aware of your "chase": your chase for pleasure, for happiness, for knowledge, for certainty, etc.

 Give your full attention to the present moment. Remember this moment is fine, and precious.

DONT'S

 Don't escape the moment. Don't look at your smartphone. Just be. And chill. Inner peace is just around the corner.

 Don't fill your brain with junk: junk news, junk foods, gossip, etc. Be at peace with "now".

 Don't take life for granted. Realize the ordinary can be extraordinary.

part 26

meaning

The final step of inner peace is moving in the right
direction. The more clarity you have,
the less overwhelmed you'll be.

Inner peace through meaning

PURPOSE, MEANING

<u>Viktor Frankl</u>, a Holocaust survivor, endured horrific conditions in concentration camps. Yet, he found inner peace.

Frankl noticed some prisoners giving up, losing hope. He realized happiness wasn't the goal, but finding meaning in any situation.

He focused on small things - a mental picture of his wife, finishing a task well. These tiny anchors kept him grounded. Even in the darkest times, Frankl chose his attitude.

He discovered inner peace wasn't about comfort, but choosing purpose over despair.

Expecting leads to
suffering. Accepting
leads to meaning.
Maxime Lagacé

no struggle, no meaning

You have to do hard things to
create your own meaning in
life. Naval Ravikant

We are all stumblers, and the
beauty and meaning of life are
in the stumbling. David Brooks

You can seek the comfortable
or the meaningful. Choose
wisely. Maxime Lagacé

Sometimes, the simple things are more fun and meaningful than all the banquets in the world.
E.A. Bucchianeri

no pain, no strength

FIND MEANING
Life without pain has no meaning.
Arthur Schopenhauer

FIND PEACE
The purpose of life is to find a
mode of being that's so
meaningful that the fact that life
is suffering is no longer relevant.
Jordan Peterson

KEEP GOING
Life becomes meaningful when
you work on it. You are the only
person who can make it
meaningful for yourself. Yoko Ono

The meaning of
life is to give life
a meaning.

a better person

Each person's task in life is to become
an increasingly better person.

Leo Tolstoy

only you

Sing the song that only you can sing, write the book that only you can write, build the product that only you can build... live the life that only you can live.

Naval Ravikant

3 things in life

Three things in life – your health, your mission,
and the people you love. That's it.

Naval Ravikant

do good

Happiness springs from doing good and helping others. Plato

The meaning of life is to find your gift. The purpose of life is to give it away. David Viscott

The man who is born with a talent which he is meant to use, finds his greatest happiness in using it. Johann Wolfgang von Goethe

THINK ABOUT THAT

We are here for one hundred years at the very most. During that period we must try to do something good, something useful, with our lives. If you contribute to other people's happiness, you will find the true meaning of life. 14th Dalai Lama

If we are facing in the right direction, all we have to do is keep on walking. Buddhist proverb

no expectations,
no disappointments

Act without expectation. Lao
Tzu

The more you expect, the less
room there is for happiness.
Maxime Lagacé

Once you give up expectations,
you have learned to live. Osho

There are two ways to be. One
is at war with reality and the
other is at peace. Byron Katie

key takeaways

DO'S

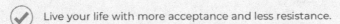 Live your life with more acceptance and less resistance.

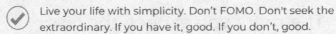 Live your life with simplicity. Don't FOMO. Don't seek the extraordinary. If you have it, good. If you don't, good.

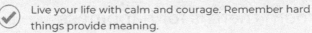 Live your life with calm and courage. Remember hard things provide meaning.

DONT'S

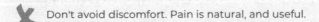 Don't avoid discomfort. Pain is natural, and useful.

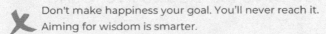 Don't make happiness your goal. You'll never reach it. Aiming for wisdom is smarter.

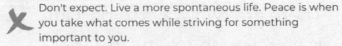 Don't expect. Live a more spontaneous life. Peace is when you take what comes while striving for something important to you.

thank you

Thank you for reading. It means a lot to know you persevered through this
book. Finding inner peace is a journey, and while I may not have all the
answers, I hope this offered some helpful insights. Remember, acceptance
and a constructive attitude can go a long way. After all, life itself is a gift.

Maxime Lagacé

call to action

WISDOMQUOTES.COM

If you like this book, and if you want to find more quotes and ideas, visit our website today. You'll find the wisdom of the best thinkers from the last 2000 years, from Buddha to Rumi, Einstein, Osho, Plato, and more.

visit wisdomquotes.com

SHOW YOU CARE

The best way to support my work is to donate. This will help me build better books and a better website. By donating, you'll also contribute to something bigger than yourself: the spread of wisdom to the world.

buymeacoffee.com/wisdomquotes

DAILY QUOTES

Do you want to receive daily wisdom quotes in your inbox? Subscribe to our newsletter today. It takes 1 minute of your time for your daily dose of wisdom, happiness, and inner peace.

wisdomquotes.com/quote-of-the-day/

Made in the USA
Monee, IL
31 October 2024

69061206R00193